Journeys through God's Word

An Introductory Course:

GENESIS

Study Guide

Scharlemann

CPH
SAINT LOUIS

Contents

Edited by Thomas J. Doyle

This publication is available in braille and in large print for the visually impaired. Write to the Library for the Blind, 1333 S. Kirkwood Rd., St. Louis, MO 63122-7295; or call 1-800-433-3954.

Maps/charts taken from *The NIV Study Bible*. Copyright © 1985 by The Zondervan Corporation. Used by permission of Zondervan Publishing House.

Scripture quotations are taken from the HOLY BIBLE: NEW INTERNATIONAL VERSION®. NIV®. Copyright © 1973, 1978, 1984 by International Bible Society. Used by permission of Zondervan Publishing House. All rights reserved.

Copyright © 1998 Concordia Publishing House
3558 South Jefferson Avenue, St. Louis, MO 63118-3968
Manufactured in the United States of America.

Introduction

The study of the Old Testament is nothing less than an exploration into the thoughts of God and His desires for ordinary people like you and me. It takes us from this hardened and selfish world into the promise of a world where God's peace, justice, and mercy will be complete.

Delving into the Bible for the first time can be somewhat intimidating. We are taken to a distant past that is full of unfamiliar customs and traditions. We must become acquainted with a nation that viewed the world differently than many people do today. And we must begin to alter some of our current definitions to grasp the full meaning of our Lord's love and compassion.

As foreign as many customs and traditions might seem to us today, we will discover that the nature of the human race remains the same. We are trapped today—as people were centuries ago—in an imperfect world where evil and pain seem all too prevalent. We, too, can view the world as meaningless and without hope. But Jesus Christ came to rescue the world from its quagmire, and His deliverance continues to change our lives. Pray that the Word of God, as it comes to you in this study, will begin to alter your perspective. May His promises give you rich and lasting hope and joy!

How to Use This Study

The Study Guide will direct your study of Genesis. The typical lesson is divided into five parts:

1. Approaching This Study
2. An Overview
3. Working with the Text
4. Applying the Message
5. Taking the Message Home

"Approaching This Study" is intended to whet the reader's appetite for the topics at hand. It leads participants into the world of the Old Testament while summarizing the issues to be examined. "An Overview" summarizes the textual material used in each lesson. Before the text is examined in detail, it is viewed as a whole, allowing participants to "see the forest" before "exploring the trees." "Working with the Text" draws participants into deeper biblical study, encouraging them to discover the gems of universal truth that lie in the details of God's Word. When questions appear difficult or unclear, the Leaders Guide provides answers to help in the discussion. "Applying the Message" leads participants from the recorded Word of God to its possible application in their present lives. It helps participants more fully realize the implications of God's Word for the daily experience of a Christian. Finally, "Taking the Message Home" invites participants to continue their scriptural meditation at home. Suggestions are given for personal reflection, for private study of topics raised by the session, and for preparation for the upcoming session. The study of God's Word will be greatly enhanced by those actively pursuing the suggestions offered in this section.

Each session ends with some "trivia"—interesting facts about Bible times—under "Did You Know That ...?" This is intended to spark interest and generate additional discussion and can be used to develop inquisitiveness and enthusiasm about related issues ripe for exploration.

A glossary is provided at the end of the Study Guide. Because a study of the Old Testament will include language that may occasionally seem foreign and difficult, the glossary will help participants become more comfortable with terms, phrases, and customs in the Christian church. It will also help explain how biblical concepts such as love and grace may differ from current worldly definitions.

The Study Guide incorporates easy-to-read charts and maps that will aid participants in their understanding of biblical geography and chronology. These should be referred to frequently, as they give visual support to the context of the sessions.

Session 1

Where Did It All Come From?

Genesis 1–4

Approaching This Study

Genesis is a book of beginnings and promises. It explains the beginning of the universe, the beginning of humankind, the beginning of sin, the beginning of God's people, the beginning of God's covenant promises with Abraham and his descendants, and the beginning of sacrifice as the substitution of death for life. The rest of the Bible—particularly the mission and ministry of Jesus Christ—only makes sense when we understand these important beginnings.

Genesis explores five great epochs revolving around individuals who received the promises of God. The first great period involves Adam and Eve, who received the promise of a Savior from sin. The second era involves Noah. He received the promise of deliverance from worldwide destruction. The third age revolves around Abraham and Sarah, who received the promises of innumerable descendants and a special land in which those descendants would dwell. The fourth era includes Abraham's son and grandson, Isaac and Jacob. They both inherited the promises given Abraham. The fifth and final period concerns one of Jacob's sons, Joseph. Not only did Joseph receive the promise of God's unwavering care and protection, but he lived to see the fulfillment of that promise.

In this first session we will investigate the origin of the universe, the creation of people, and the introduction of sin and its consequences to God's world. From God's Holy Word all things are called into existence. God's breath gives life to Adam. God appoints Adam the steward of His perfect world. But the devil enters God's perfect creation and seduces Adam and Eve with lies and deception. Adam and Eve fall for the devil's lies. Sin enters the world. All people must forever suffer the temporal consequences of sin. Without these initial understandings about creation and sin, the purpose of Jesus' person and work would be unappreciated. We could never understand our desperate need for Jesus' sacrificial death.

An Overview

Unit Reading

Genesis is an engaging book composed of numerous interesting and entertaining narratives. Before continuing with this session, read Genesis 1–4 from a modern, easy-to-understand version of the Bible. To make this reading even more enjoyable, volunteers may choose to read one of the following parts: the narrator, the voice of God, Adam, Eve, the serpent, Cain, and Lamech.

The Message in Brief

The word *genesis* means "beginning." As you read these first four chapters, explain in your own words how each of the following beginnings took place:

1. The beginning of the universe:

2. The beginning of people:

3. The beginning of sin:

4. The beginning of pain and toil:

5. The beginning of death:

6. The beginning of murder:

7. The beginning of the city (Genesis 4:17):

8. The beginning of God's salvation promises (Genesis 3:15):

Working with the Text

The Origin of the Universe (Genesis 1:1–2:3)

1. Of all biblical narratives, the creation account is one of the most familiar. Let's look at some of the things we can learn about God in the creation event found in Genesis 1. For example, can you find evidence of the Trinity (that is, God being "three persons in one God") already in verses 1–3 of the first chapter? Read John 1:1–14 for some help! Then look at Genesis 1:26 and find the words that also support evidence of the Trinity.

> In the beginning was the Word, and the Word was with God, and the Word was God. He was with God in the beginning. Through Him all things were made; without Him nothing was made that has been made. In Him was life, and that life was the light of men. The light shines in the darkness, but the darkness has not understood it. There came a man who was sent from God; his

name was John. He came as a witness to testify concerning that light, so that through him all men might believe. He himself was not the light; he came only as a witness to the light. The true light that gives light to every man was coming into the world. He was in the world, and though the world was made through Him, the world did not recognize Him. He came to that which was His own, but His own did not receive Him. Yet to all who received Him, to those who believed in His name, He gave the right to become children of God—children born not of natural descent, nor of human decision or a husband's will, but born of God. The Word became flesh and made His dwelling among us. We have seen His glory, the glory of the One and Only, who came from the Father, full of grace and truth. (John 1:1–14)

2. Who named the day and the night, the sky, and the land and the seas? How is God's power to name significant? What is the significance of people's ability to name their children or their pets (or in some cases, their cars!)?

3. Consider the diet of people and animals in Eden. Describe their food supply according to Genesis 1:29–31. What does this suggest about the food chain as we know it today? How does God continue to describe His creation?

4. What did God do on the seventh day of creation? How would

God's seventh-day rest become the foundation of the Sabbath celebration according to Exodus 20:8–11? And to whom would the Sabbath point according to Colossians 2:16–17?

> "Remember the Sabbath day by keeping it holy. Six days you shall labor and do all your work, but the seventh day is a Sabbath to the LORD your God. On it you shall not do any work, neither you, nor your son or daughter, nor your manservant or maidservant, nor your animals, nor the alien within your gates. For in six days the LORD made the heavens and the earth, the sea, and all that is in them, but He rested on the seventh day. Therefore the LORD blessed the Sabbath day and made it holy." (Exodus 20:8–11)

> Therefore do not let anyone judge you by what you eat or drink, or with regard to a religious festival, a New Moon celebration or a Sabbath day. These are a shadow of the things that were to come; the reality, however, is found in Christ. (Colossians 2:16–17)

The Origin of People (Genesis 2:4–25)

1. How was the earth watered according to Genesis 2:5–6? How does this indicate the perfection of God's creation?

2. Describe how God brought life to Adam. How about Eve? How are people different from God's other creatures? What does this suggest about God's unique relationship to men and women? Notice that God commanded Adam to name all the animals. Again, what does this suggest about the unique nature of people?

3. Describe the one restriction God gave to Adam and Eve in Eden. From what tree did God forbid them to eat? What would happen if they ate the fruit from the forbidden tree?

The Origin and Consequences of Sin (Genesis 3:1–4:26)

1. Focus on the serpent's deception in Genesis 3:1–5. Discuss the various tactics used by the serpent to entice Eve into sin. What do you think ultimately motivated Eve to eat the fruit? Why?

2. Describe the manner in which Adam and Eve attempted to excuse their sinful behavior. How do people frequently use the same excuse today?

3. Describe the curses given Adam and Eve. How do they remain relevant today? How was the curse against the serpent's offspring by Eve's descendant the first promise about Jesus Christ?

4. What evidence can you provide that Adam passed sin to his sons? How is the curse of sin evident in Cain's great, great, great, grandson Lamech?

5. How does God demonstrate His grace (His undeserved love and favor) in Adam and Eve's exile from Eden according to Genesis 3:21–24?

Applying the Message

1. After witnessing the manner in which God created all things, what does it mean to you when John's gospel refers to Jesus as "the Word"?

2. What are the implications of inheriting sin? Can anyone live a perfect life? As cute as infants may be, what truth does Scripture teach us about their spiritual nature?

3. Consider Adam and Eve's motivation for eating the fruit from the tree of the knowledge of good and evil. In what ways do you think the motive to sin is always the same?

4. Consider the consequences suffered by Adam and Eve after they sinned. Suddenly they realized they were naked. They experienced shame and hid themselves from God. How do the consequences of sin affect people in the same way today?

Taking the Message Home

Review

Spend an hour in a park or walking around your neighborhood and reflect on God's creation. During this hour of reflection, jot down all those things that underscore the beauty, majesty, and power of God's creative activity. Then jot down evidence of sin's corrupting effects on God's creation. Be prepared to share these observations at the next session.

Looking Ahead

In the next session we will learn about Noah and the worldwide flood. Read Genesis 5–7 before your next meeting. Be particularly aware of the sin that broke the camel's back, so to speak, provoking God's judgment against the world.

Working Ahead

Select one or more of the following activities to complete before the next session:

1. If you can discover the roots of your family, be prepared to share with others your family's history. From which part of the world did your ancestors originate? Do you know any interesting stories about members of your family tree? What are the implications of knowing we are all descendants of Noah?

2. As you contemplate the story of the flood, consider how God used Noah and his family to deliver not only themselves from destruction, but also the species of the earth. How does this provide a model for our stewardship of God's creation today? In what ways should we protect God's creatures from extinction today?

3. Read 1 Peter 3:18–22. How does Peter equate Baptism to Noah's ark? How is Baptism an act of deliverance from certain destruction?

Did You Know That ... ?

According to the directions found in Genesis 2:10–14, the Garden of Eden must have been located near the Persian Gulf by the present-day borders of Iran, Iraq, and Kuwait. We will never find it because the Lord has placed his angels to guard its entrance. We can only have access to the tree of life through God's redemption in Jesus Christ. The tree of life is presented again at the end of the Bible, bringing a closure to God's revelation. The tree of life is growing in the new Jerusalem, our heavenly home (Revelation 22:1–2).

The Genealogy
of Genesis 1–4

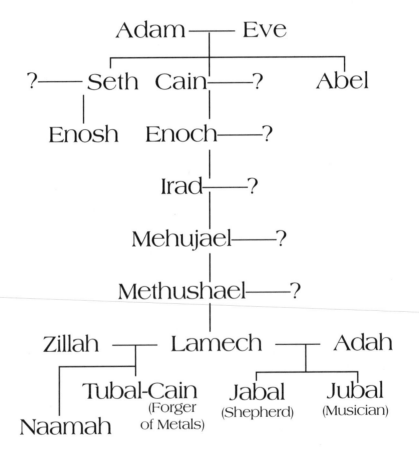

Session 2

A Worldwide Flood

Genesis 5–7

Approaching This Study

In our last session, Genesis 4 presented a genealogy from Cain to Lamech. Today's session follows the genealogy beginning from Adam and Eve's other son, Seth. Although Cain's descendants continued to disobey the Lord, Seth's descendants were generally God-fearing.

Noah descended from Seth's line. As we study Seth's genealogy, we'll discover that many of his descendants' names are similar to the names of Cain's descendants. Cain's descendants and Seth's descendants almost appear to form parallel genealogies. One group turns away from God, while the other respects and loves the Lord. These "parallel lines" give us an important clue about the reason for God's angry judgment unleashed by the flood.

In the account of the flood, God discloses His covenant promise to Noah. He will deliver Noah and his family from certain destruction, and, Noah, acting on God's behalf, will keep the animals of the world from extinction. Just as Adam and Eve were stewards of God's garden, so Noah and his family would preserve and govern God's creatures.

In the flood, God initiates the biblical theme of "the remnant." In each period of world history, God intervenes to protect and redeem a remnant of His faithful people. A remnant reflects faithfulness to God's Word when the rest of the world has turned to false gods. After the floods, God would choose Abraham and his descendants as the remnant of His people. After Abraham's descendants failed God, they were delivered into exile. A remnant would return to the Promised Land and start again. With the coming of Jesus, only a remnant of the Jews would follow Christ and find eternal salvation. The members of the Christian church are the remnant of God's faithful people today.

An Overview

Unit Reading

Genesis 5 is difficult to read because it includes a series of names that are difficult to pronounce. Do your best as you read this chapter aloud. Volunteers should read aloud chapters 6 and 7, too.

The Message in Brief

As Seth's descendants enjoy long lives, the world becomes more populated. But as the population increases, so does the world's evil. Finally, the Lord loses patience with His creatures, condemning all of them except Noah and his family to a watery grave. The Lord desires to start over with His creation. God warns Noah about the upcoming destruction and commands him to build an ark within which Noah will house his family and a pair of each of the world's animals. Noah believes the Lord and trusts in His promise. God delivers Noah and his family from destruction.

Working with the Text

From Adam to Noah (Genesis 5)

1. How long do each of Seth's descendants live?

Enosh _____

Kenan _____

Mahalalel _____

Jared _____

Enoch _____

Methuselah _____

Lamech _____

2. One cannot read the names of Seth's descendants without recognizing their similarity to the names of Cain's descendants. Draw a line connecting the names of Seth's descendants to the names of Cain's descendants that resemble them:

Cain's descendants	Seth's descendants
Enoch	Enosh

Irad	Kenan
Mehujael	Mahalalel
Methushael	Jared
Lamech	Enoch
	Methuselah
	Lamech

Cain's descendant, Lamech, was a polygamist and a murderer, while Seth's descendant, Lamech, was Noah's father. What might the author suggest by recording these parallel lineages?

Building the Ark (Genesis 6)

1. How might the parallel lineages established in Genesis 5 help us interpret what is meant when the writer describes the "sons of God" marrying the "daughters of men" in Genesis 6:1–2? How did God respond to these intermarriages? What would happen to people's life spans as a result of this sin?

2. Write the dimensions of the ark. Try to compare the size of the ark with some familiar object in today's world. How many decks did the ark contain?

3. What kind of covenant did God establish with Noah? Who would God protect from the upcoming flood? What was Noah's responsibility toward God? How many of each kind of animal did Noah bring on board?

4. What would have happened if Noah had not believed the Lord's warning and promise? How does this demonstrate God's ability to "save through faith"?

The Flood (Genesis 7)

1. Actually, Noah occasionally brought more than just a pair of each animal species on board. According to 7:2–3, how many clean animals and birds did Noah rescue? Why did Noah bring a few extra of these creatures on board (look up 8:20)?

2. How old was Noah when the rain began? From what two sources did the waters emerge according to 7:11?

3. For how many days did the waters rise? According to Exodus 24:18, how many days did Moses spend on Mt. Sinai when he received the Ten Commandments? According to Numbers 14:33, how long would God's people wander in the wilderness before entering the Promised Land? According to 2 Samuel 5:4, how long did King David reign? According to Jonah 3:4, how many days would God wait for the city of Nineveh to repent before He would destroy it? And how long did Jesus fast in the wilderness according to Matthew 4:2? What does all this suggest to you about the way God's Word connects generations of believers?

Then Moses entered the cloud as he went on up the mountain.

And he stayed on the mountain forty days and forty nights. (Exodus 24:18)

"Your children will be shepherds here for forty years, suffering for your unfaithfulness, until the last of your bodies lies in the desert." (Numbers 14:33)

David was thirty years old when he became king, and he reigned forty years. (2 Samuel 5:4)

On the first day, Jonah started into the city. He proclaimed: "Forty more days and Nineveh will be overturned." (Jonah 3:4)

After fasting forty days and forty nights, He was hungry. (Matthew 4:2)

Applying the Message

1. Share with others an episode when you felt overwhelmed by a flood of life's problems. Read 1 Corinthians 10:13. How might God's promise act as an ark during your flood?

No temptation has seized you except what is common to man. And God is faithful; He will not let you be tempted beyond what you can bear. But when you are tempted, He will also provide a way out so that you can stand up under it. (1 Corinthians 10:13)

2. Isn't it amazing to read about the life spans of God's early people? As people continued to disobey the Lord, their life spans shortened. Why is it reasonable to assume we will live longer, healthier, more fulfilling lives if we follow God's will than if we disobey? What does this suggest about God's commands?

3. What kind of response do you think the building of the ark aroused in Noah's neighbors? In what ways do people continue to scoff at those who trust in the promises of God?

Taking the Message Home

Review

Take a few minutes to read 1 Peter 3:18–22 and reflect on God's use of water. How did God use it to purge the world of evil during the flood? How does Peter relate the flood to the purging of sin and evil through Holy Baptism? How does this suggest that Holy Baptism is much more than a mere symbol of God's grace?

Looking Ahead

Before the next session read Genesis 9:1–3. God's command to Noah sounds very much like His command to Adam and Eve in Genesis 1:28–30. Reflect on how this similarity demonstrates God's intent to start His creation anew.

Working Ahead

Select one or more of the following activities to complete before the next session:

1. One of the universal symbols of peace is the dove with an olive branch in its mouth. Read Genesis 8:11 and consider the source of this symbol and how it came to represent peace.

2. In Genesis 5:1–3 we are reminded that God created Adam and Eve in His image, that is, perfectly in tune with God's will. But after Adam and Eve sinned, Seth was conceived and born in the image of fallen Adam. What does this suggest to you about God's plan to start over with Noah and his family? Do you think this will rid the world of sin? Why not?

3. Try to remember the most impressive rainbow you've ever seen. Describe the situation. God promised Noah He would never again destroy the world in a flood, and the sign of His promise would be the rainbow. Make a mental note to remember this promise when you see a rainbow.

Did You Know That ... ?

Many cultures around the world possess legends about the flood:

- Egyptians have a legend that the earth was cleansed of wickedness by a great flood; only a few shepherds escaped.

- In Hindu tradition, a man named Manu is warned about an upcoming flood. He builds a ship and is delivered from a deluge that destroys every other creature.

- In Chinese tradition, the founder of Chinese civilization, Fa-He escapes from a flood that has been sent because people have rebelled against heaven. He, his wife, his three sons, and three daughters are saved!

- The Druids in England carried a legend that the world was repopulated from a righteous patriarch who was saved from a flood in a strong ship. The flood had been sent to destroy the world for its evil ways.

- The Polynesians have legends of a flood; only eight people escaped.

- The Mexican legend states that one man, his wife, and his children were delivered from a worldwide flood in a ship.

- The Peruvians believe that one man and one woman were saved in a box that floated on the waters of a great flood.

- The Native Americans have various legends about one, three, or eight people saved in a boat that floated on floodwaters above a high mountain.

- A legend in Greenland claims that the earth once tilted over and the peoples of the world were drowned, except for one man and one woman who repopulated the earth.

- And in the archives of the Temple of Marduk, in Babylon, these words are related by Berosus, from 300 B.C.: "Xisuthros, a king, was warned by one of the gods to build a ship, and take into it friends and relatives and all different kinds of animals, with all necessary food. Whereupon he built an immense ship, which was stranded in Armenia. Upon subsidence of the Flood, he sent out birds; the third time, they returned not. He came out, built an altar, and sacrificed!"

(From *Halley's Bible Handbook* by Henry H. Halley, [Grand Rapids, Mich.: Zondervan Publishing House, 1965), p. 75. Used by permission.)

Why should these various legends from around the world amaze us? We are all descendants of Noah!

The Genealogy
of Genesis 1–5

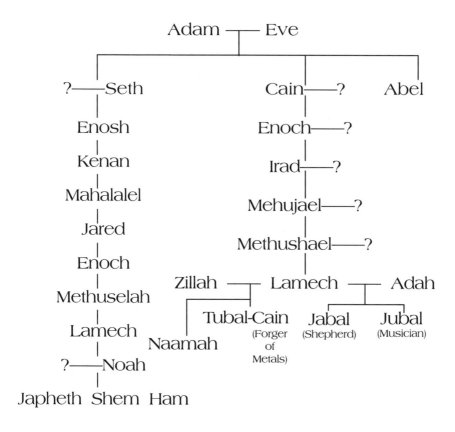

Adam —— Eve

?——Seth   Cain——?   Abel

Enosh   Enoch——?

Kenan   Irad——?

Mahalalel   Mehujael——?

Jared   Methushael——?

Enoch   Zillah —— Lamech —— Adah

Methuselah   Tubal-Cain   Jabal   Jubal

Lamech   Naamah   (Forger   (Shepherd)   (Musician)
                              of
?——Noah   Metals)

Japheth Shem Ham

Session 3

A New Beginning

Genesis 8–10

Approaching This Study

For nearly half a year the floodwaters rolled across the surface of our planet without receding. And during these 150 days, God's name is only mentioned in the phrase "but God remembered Noah" (8:1). Perhaps Noah didn't even hear from Him during this frightening period. Can you imagine floating on waters that covered the earth—an endless sea of water—without any possible land upon which to rest for 150 days? What a test of faith! Noah, his family, and the chosen animals remained one small dot on an earth covered with water.

When Noah noticed the waters receding, he began sending out a few of his birds to see whether they would return to the ark or settle on dry land. Finally, one of his doves returned with an olive branch in its mouth—proof of dry land. When the bird was once again released, it never returned. After the waters receded, Noah, his family, and the animals of the ark began God's creation anew, living under the covenant of the rainbow, which symbolized God's promise never again to destroy the world in a flood.

But, of course, Noah and his family were tainted with original sin. It would not be long before God's people again violated His will. Through Noah's children, the world began to repopulate, spreading throughout the areas we know as the Near East, Egypt, and southern Europe. As the population increased, so did sin and corruption. But God would keep His promise—a promise first made to Adam and Eve—a promise of a Savior who would rescue people from sin and its ultimate consequence, death.

An Overview

Unit Reading

Read Genesis 8 and 9. These chapters recount Noah's deliverance from the flood and God's new covenant with His people. Pay particular attention to those words or phrases spoken by God that are similar to the words He spoke to Adam and Eve. We will examine selected verses from this chapter later in this session.

The Message in Brief

Genesis 8–10 takes the reader from the flood to right before the building of the Tower of Babel. As is true of so much of Scripture, this section depicts the grace and forgiveness of God toward His people. God fulfills one covenant made to Noah (to rescue Noah from the flood) and initiates another (that He will never again destroy the earth with a flood). But despite God's providential care and love, Noah and his family quickly slide into sinful behavior. Although God has given His world a new start, the consequences of sin remain. And as the world's population increases and people spread throughout the world, wickedness expands as well.

Working with the Text

The Waters Recede (Genesis 8)

1. The Hebrew words for *wind* and *spirit* are the same. Knowing this, compare Genesis 8:1 with 1:2. What similarity do you find? Also compare 8:5 with 1:9 and 8:17 with 1:22. What do these similarities suggest?

2. Olive trees will not grow in higher elevations. So even though the waters had sufficiently receded to reveal some of the mountaintops, what important information would the dove with an olive leaf in its mouth suggest? When Noah released the dove a second time, it never returned. What does this tell us?

3. Even though the swelling floods rose over a period of 40 days, we might be curious how long Noah and his crew remained on the ark before they could once again inhabit the earth. Compare Genesis 7:11 with 8:13–14. Can you determine from these two references the length of time between the beginning of the flood and Noah's departure from the ark?

4. What was the first thing Noah did after freeing the animals from the ark? This isn't the first reference to a sacrifice. Cain and Abel also offered sacrifices to the Lord. Refer back to Genesis 4:3–5. What do you think makes a sacrifice pleasing to the Lord?

A New Covenant (Genesis 9)

1. How does the Lord indicate He knows about the existence and implications of original sin in Genesis 8:21? How does this sin manifest itself in the story of Noah in chapter 9? What does this tell you about the future of God's people? Of Noah's three sons, who was the most culpable? And who will descend from him? What will happen to his descendants according to Genesis 9:25–27?

2. Compare Genesis 9:1–2 with 1:28. How does God's command to Noah indicate His hope for a new beginning? How does God modify His command to Noah from His original command to Adam and Eve (Genesis 9:3)?

3. Even though people were now given permission to kill and eat animals, what would be the penalty for murdering another human being (Genesis 9:6)?

4. God created a new covenant with Noah, his descendants, and all the creatures of the earth. God's new covenant was unilateral and unconditional. Only God was active. What did God promise He would never do again? Describe the sign of that covenant.

The "Table of Nations" (Genesis 10)

1. Chapter 10 consists of three main divisions giving the genealogy for each of Noah's three sons. According to 10:5, what happened to some of Japheth's descendants? The descendants of Ham settled in ominous areas of the world, including Assyria, Shinar (Babylonia), and Canaan. Throughout their history, God's people would battle and conquer the tribes inhabiting the land of Canaan. How does the curse against Ham's son, Canaan, suggest this future? The descendants of Shem would become known as Semites. In what context have you heard this word before? In 10:24 we discover that one of Shem's great grandsons would be named Eber. This is the root word for *Hebrew*.

2. As you read about the territory of the Canaanite people, perhaps two well-known cities stand out. Look at verse 19 and list the two cities familiar to most people today. How are they remembered?

Applying the Message

1. God made a covenant with Adam and Eve, promising He would conquer the serpent through one of Eve's descendants. With Noah, God promised deliverance from the flood and made a covenant never destroy earthly life with a flood. God's history with His people involves covenants. Summarize the covenant God has made with you. Read John 3:16, 36; 5:24; and 6:47.

"For God so loved the world that He gave His one and only Son, that whoever believes in Him shall not perish but have eternal life." (John 3:16)

"Whoever believes in the Son has eternal life, but whoever rejects the Son will not see life, for God's wrath remains on him." (John 3:36)

"I tell you the truth, whoever hears My word and believes Him who sent Me has eternal life and will not be condemned; he has crossed over from death to life." (John 5:24)

"I tell you the truth, he who believes has everlasting life." (John 6:47)

2. God told Noah that "every inclination of [a person's] heart is evil from childhood" (8:21). This is quite a judgment! Give some examples that support the premise that people are innately evil.

3. Having witnessed God's actions toward Adam, Eve, and Noah, how would you describe Him so far? Write some qualities that Scripture reveals that God possesses.

4. When God permitted people to eat meat and fish as sources of food, He warned Noah not to eat meat that still had its lifeblood in it (9:4). Why was this important? Compare Genesis 9:4 with Leviticus 17:10–14, and notice how God connected blood with life. Even though the lifeblood of animals was not to be eaten, the same blood was important for sacrifices. It made "atonement" for life, that is, it made amends for a sinful life, trading a life for a life. How might you view Jesus' death on the cross as such a sacrifice?

> "[Say to them:] 'Any Israelite or any alien living among them who eats any blood—I will set my face against that person who eats blood and will cut him off from his people. For the life of a creature is in the blood, and I have given it to you to make atonement for yourselves on the altar; it is the blood that makes atonement for one's life. Therefore I say to the Israelites, "None of you may eat blood, nor may an alien living among you eat blood."

> " 'Any Israelite or any alien living among you who hunts any animal or bird that may be eaten must drain out the blood and cover it with earth, because the life of every creature is its blood. That is why I have said to the Israelites, "You must not eat the blood of any creature, because the life of every creature is its blood; anyone who eats it must be cut off."' " (Leviticus 17:10–14)

Taking the Message Home

Review

Reflect on the manner in which God supplied Noah with abundant grace, love, and care. In return, Noah became drunk, leading himself and his children into sin. Does this sad story continue in our lives? In what ways are you blessed by God? And yet, how do you sometimes treat God's will and Word? Praise God for His ongoing forgiveness through faith in Jesus Christ!

Looking Ahead

In the next session we begin the third great epoch of the Genesis story. From all the peoples of the world, God will choose Abram to be the father of His people. When God chooses Abram, Abram responds in faith to God's commands. But just as Noah had his weaknesses, so Abram will demonstrate His own sinful frailty. Sometimes his faith is weak. Sometimes He will behave in a cowardly fashion. Read Genesis 12:10–13. How would you describe Abram's behavior in this passage? What does this suggest about our thoughts, words, and actions?

Working Ahead

Select one or more of the following activities to complete before the next session:

1. Have you ever been "called" by God to another area of the country? You may not have heard His voice, but circumstances or opportunities led you to pack everything and move. What circumstances surrounded your decision? Describe some of the challenges and the manner in which these were resolved. Looking back, how do you see the hand of God at work?

2. Read Genesis 11:1–9. What did people try to do when they built the Tower of Babel? List various methods by which people try to "make a name for themselves" today.

3. Abram is called by God to live in the land of the Canaanites. This land would later be known as Israel. When a famine arose in the land, Abram traveled to Egypt to find life and sustenance. Later, Abram and his household would return to Israel. Read Matthew 2:13–21 and compare Abram's journey to the journey of Jesus and His family. Many Old Testament people "prefigure" Jesus Christ; that is, they create a model or pattern for the person and work of Jesus.

Did You Know That ... ?

In the "Table of Nations" detailed in Genesis 10, 14 nations arise from Japheth, 30 stem from Ham, and 26 come from Shem. These nations total 70. Frequently, the Bible uses numbers to carry a message. Both the number 7 and the number 10 are used to convey the idea of completeness. Since 70 is a multiple of 10 and 7, the number of nations arising from Japheth, Ham, and Shem denote the totality of the world's population.

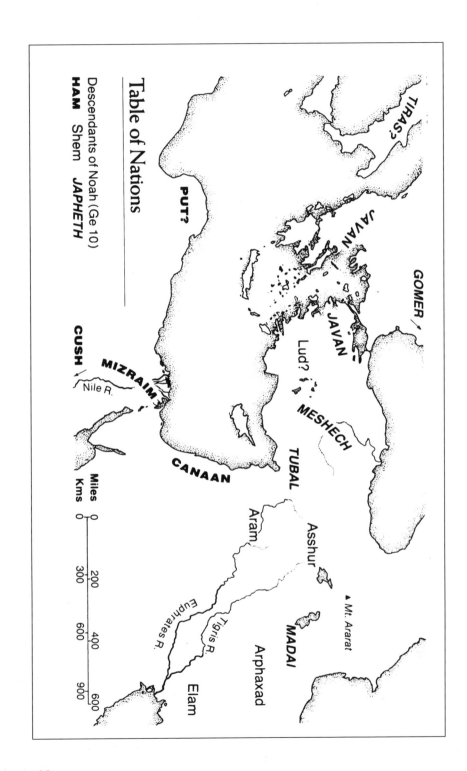

Table of Nations

Descendants of Noah (Ge 10)

HAM   Shem   *JAPHETH*

PUT?

CUSH

MIZRAIM

Nile R.

CANAAN

TIRAS?

JAVAN

GOMER

JAVAN

Lud?

MESHECH

TUBAL

Aram

Asshur

▲ Mt. Ararat

MADAI

Arphaxad

Euphrates R.

Tigris R.

Elam

| Miles | 0 | 200 | 400 | 600 |
| Kms | 0 | 300 | 600 | 900 |

Session 4

God Chooses Abram

Genesis 11–14

Approaching This Study

Genesis 10 led us through a genealogy arising from Noah's sons. Genesis 11 repeats the genealogy of Shem's descendants and extends it to Abram. These genealogies demonstrate the Lord's ongoing faithfulness to His promises.

We learned in chapter 10 that two sons were born to Shem's descendant, Eber. One was named Peleg and the other Joktan. Genesis 10's genealogy follows the line of Joktan, but the genealogy of chapter 11 follows the line of Peleg. From Peleg's line God raised up the father of the nation of Israel. His name was Abram. But notice in Genesis 10:25 that when Peleg and Joktan lived "the earth was divided." That's the reason for Peleg's name. Peleg means "division," and it's likely his name refers to the fascinating episode surrounding the Tower of Babel. The story of the Tower of Babel not only gives an explanation for the many languages of the world, but it also provides an interesting interlude between the genealogies of Genesis 10 and 11.

With the call of Abram, a new epoch began. We observe Abram traveling from his homeland of Ur of the Chaldeans into the land of Canaan upon the Lord's command. In faith, Abram believed the Lord's promise and followed His commands. In return God promised Abram innumerable descendants who would create a great nation that would dwell in the land of the Canaanites. One of the important family members who accompanied Abram was his nephew Lot. Although both Abram and Lot were from the line of Shem, God graced Abram with His covenant-promises, while Lot, through two incestuous relationships, became the father of the Ammonite and Moabite tribes. These tribes would become bitter enemies of Abram's descendants, the people of Israel. Only Abram's descendants would be God's light in an increasingly pagan world.

An Overview

Unit Reading

Even though four chapters may seem like a great deal of material to read, it will seem like enjoyable storytelling because most of it is narrative. Let one volunteer read Genesis 11:1–9. Then let some brave soul finish the chapter. It is perfectly acceptable to pronounce the names incorrectly! A third volunteer can read Genesis 12 and 13. When a volunteer reads chapter 14, verses 1–10 may be omitted.

The Message in Brief

The chapters in this session's readings are important because they depict the founding of God's people under Abram. Abram receives a promise that God would create a great nation. Abram's descendants would live in the land of Canaan. This land would become known as the "Promised Land." Through Abram's descendants, God would create the nation of Israel. They would be chosen as God's light to the people to reflect God's love, justice, and mercy to a fallen, idolatrous world.

Because the nation of Israel would fail in its task, God would send a new and true "Israel" in His Son, Jesus Christ. Jesus would fulfill what Abram's descendants were unable to fulfill. All people today who trust in Jesus' death and resurrection for their salvation are now considered God's chosen people. As Paul says in Galatians 3:29, "If you belong to Christ, then you are Abraham's seed, and heirs according to the promise."

Working with the Text

The Tower of Confusion (Genesis 11:1–9)

1. What motivations lie behind the building of the Tower of Babel? How are these sinful motivations still evident today?

2. Now read Genesis 28:10–13. Who creates the "stairway" between heaven and earth? And who creates this link between man and God according to 1 Timothy 2:5–6?

For there is one God and one mediator between God and men, the man Christ Jesus, who gave Himself as a ransom for all men—the testimony given in its proper time. (1 Timothy 2:5–6)

3. God seems concerned that if the peoples of the world succeed in building the tower, "nothing they plan to do will be impossible for them." Do you think God is threatened by their endeavors? In what way do you think His response in confusing their language might have been an act of grace rather than judgment?

From Shem to Abram (Genesis 11:10–32)

List the life spans of Shem's descendants:

Shem lived _____ years.

Arphaxad lived _____ years.

Shelah lived _____ years.

Eber lived _____ years.

Peleg lived _____ years.

Reu lived _____ years.

Serug lived _____ years.

Nahor lived _____ years.

Terah (Abram's father) lived _____ years.

What's happening to people's life spans? How is this a fulfillment of God's curse upon the wickedness of humankind before the flood (Genesis 6:1–3)?

Abram's Call (Genesis 12)

1. How many promises were given to Abram in Genesis 12:2–3? How would you summarize them? What did God command Abram to do in Genesis 12:1?

2. How old was Abram when he left Haran, and who went with him? When Abram reached Canaan, what promise did the Lord repeat? And how did Abram respond to this promise?

3. Because a famine arose in Canaan, Abram traveled to Egypt. Notice how he tells his wife, Sarai, to claim she is his sister. Why would he do this? What does this say about Abram's character—even though he is one of the great heroes of the Bible?

Not Enough Room for the Two of Them (Genesis 13)

1. Notice how Abram left Bethel in Canaan for Egypt and then returned to Bethel. Much later, who else was forced into Egypt because of a famine (Genesis 42:1–2)? As a result of their voyage, what happened to their descendants (Exodus 1:1–11)? Who led the Israelites from Egypt back to Canaan (Exodus 3:15–20)?

2. According to Genesis 13:1–2 Abram left Egypt wealthy. Because Abram and Lot possessed so many flocks and herds, they couldn't coexist in the same area. They needed more land. How did they decide on territory? Between Abram and Lot, who was the most covetous?

But who was the most faithful in trusting the Lord's providential care? Where did Lot "pitch his tents"?

Abram Rescues Lot and Meets Melchizedek (Genesis 14)

1. Because Lot had pitched his tents near Sodom, he was vulnerable to an invasion by four allied kings who wanted to plunder Sodom and Gomorrah. When Abram learned the fate of his nephew, he gathered his "army" together. How many men was Abram able to enlist? Abram attacked his enemies. Describe Abram's faith in God's providential care.

2. Out of nowhere appeared King Melchizedek. From Genesis 14:18–20 and from other Scripture passages, we know learn the following facts about Melchizedek:

   a. He was a king.

   b. He was the king of Salem.

   c. Salem would become Jerusalem. Thus, in a way, Melchizedek was "king of Jerusalem."

   d. The word *Salem* means "peace." Thus, Melchizedek was the "king of peace."

   e. Melchizedek was also a priest. He was called a "priest of God Most High" even before the priesthood under Aaron was established!

   f. The name Melchizedek literally means "king of righteousness."

g.   Melchizedek gives Abram "bread and wine."

h.   In thanksgiving, Abram gives Melchizedek a tithe, that is, a tenth of everything.

Now, of whom does Melchizedek remind you? Why?

Applying the Message

1. One of the wonderful lessons of the Tower of Babel is the futility of our attempts to storm the gates of heaven by our own efforts and achievements. In what ways do people feel they can "climb their way to heaven?" Why do you think it's so difficult for people to receive God's free gift of salvation without thinking they have to help in some way?

2. When Abram told Sarai to tell the Egyptians she was his sister, he was half right. In reality, Sarai was his half sister. But Abram wasn't being completely honest. Share an example of a situation in which your faith was compromised because of peer pressure.

3. When Lot chose the land he would inhabit, he chose the most fertile. Abram was left with the least attractive territory. In the end, Lot suffered for his greed. First, he was taken captive by invading kings. Later, he would have to flee Sodom because of God's impending judgment on the city. Give some examples of how people's greed backfires on them, that is, how greed seems to make everyone, even the greedy one, suffer.

4. To this day the Jews have a saying that when a man is killed, a whole world is exterminated. As we contemplate the nation which would arise from Abram's descendants, how much more valuable does this consideration make each human life?

5. Consider God's faithfulness to His people in spite of their sins. God remains faithful to us in spite of our unfaithfulness. How does Jesus' death on the cross and resurrection from the grave give you comfort and hope in spite of sin? Use the descriptors of Melchizedek to describe the person and work of Jesus on your behalf.

Taking the Message Home

Review

Read Hebrews 7. Notice how the author expands on the theme relating Jesus to Melchizedek. As you meditate on this chapter, consider the implications of Jesus being a completely different kind of priest than the kind with whom God's people had been familiar. In what ways is Jesus, a priest in the order of Melchizedek, different than the average priest?

Looking Ahead

Sometimes it seems that although we know we can rely on God's care and protection, He takes His time helping us! Think about Abram and Sarai. They lived under the promise of a descendant, and yet Abram was becoming an old man. He was nearing 100, and his wife was almost 90! How could they possibly trust in the Lord's promise? Share with others an episode when it seemed the Lord could not possibly help, but then He came through.

Working Ahead

Select one or more of the following activities to complete before the next session:

1. In the immediate chapters to come, God confirms His covenant promises with Abram and Sarai. As He does so, He changes their names to Abraham and Sarah. In the Bible, when one of God's people experiences a life-changing experience with the Lord, his or her name is often changed as a sign of new life. For example, Jacob's name was changed to Israel. Saul became Paul. Simon became Peter. If you were to change your name, what name would you choose? Why?

2. Look up *angel* in a Bible dictionary and discover its meaning. If possible, uncover the word's origin. What language did it come from? And what was the word in its original language?

3. Share a time when you "bargained" with God, that is, you attempted through prayer to "make deals" with God in order to get your own way. What happened? Did it work?

Did You Know That ... ?

The typical temple tower in Mesopotamia around Abraham's time was known as a ziggurat. It was square at the base and had sloping, stepped sides. On the top was a shrine. Many of these ziggurats were given names that suggest they, too, were designed to reach heaven. Names of other ziggurats uncovered by archaeologists include "The House of the Link Between Heaven and Earth," "The House of the Seven Guides of Heaven and Earth," "The House of the Foundation-Platform of Heaven and Earth," and "The House of the Mountain of the Universe."

Apparently, the Tower of Babel was the most formidable attempt to build a "staircase to heaven!"

Session 5

Abraham May Have Doubted, but God Kept Promising

Genesis 15–18

Approaching This Study

This session's chapters see-saw between God's promises and Abram's faith and doubts. Again and again the Lord returns to Abram and promises him innumerable descendants who will live in the land of Canaan. But Abram and Sarai struggle with skepticism. To dramatically illustrate His covenant, God asks Abram to collect a variety of animals and birds, which are cut in half. By crossing through these separated carcasses, God confirms His promise of a homeland for Abram's descendants. Unfortunately, as Abram and Sarai become older their doubts grow. How could the Lord fulfill His promises if the couple remained childless? In desperation Sarai and Abram turn to Sarai's maidservant, Hagar. Sure enough, Hagar gives birth to Abram's son, but this son is not the fulfillment of God's promise. As a result of Abram and Sarai's attempt to manipulate the fulfillment of God's promise, complications and difficulties arise in the relationship between Hagar, Sarai, Ishmael, and Abram. Nevertheless, God affirms His covenant with Abram through the rite of circumcision, changing Abram's name to Abraham and his wife's name to Sarah.

Doubts arise again in Abraham's and Sarah's mind, however. So the Lord appears to them accompanied by two angels and gives them the promise of a son within the year. Sarah laughs at the prospect. After all, she is 90 years old! But both Abraham and Sarah will end up learning that with God nothing is impossible.

The chapters conclude with an ominous turn. God warns Abraham that He will destroy Sodom and Gomorrah because of the cities' great acts of wickedness. Abraham is disturbed because his nephew, Lot, has settled near Sodom. He attempts to negotiate with God, hoping his relatives will be spared. God listens to Abraham and agrees to his terms.

Although Abraham's relatives will be spared, the cities will be destroyed. There simply are not enough faithful citizens remaining in the city of Sodom to assuage God's wrath.

This session focuses on the struggle between faith and unbelief. This is of great concern to us because it is a struggle Christians face. God promises His people wonderful blessings, but people wrestle with their trust in His promises. The story of Abraham and Sarah reflects the ongoing conflict within each believer's heart. As one father said when he brought his demon-possessed son to Jesus (see Mark 9:24): "I do believe; help me overcome my unbelief!"

An Overview

Unit Reading

Why not make the reading of Genesis 15–18 into a radio play? Choose one person to be the narrator. Choose others to read the parts of Abram, Sarai, God, Hagar, and the angel of the Lord. The person who reads God's part should also read the parts of the three visitors who appear at Abram's tent.

The Message in Brief

These four chapters demonstrate God's ongoing determination to fulfill His promises. God refuses to allow Abram and Sarai to lose track of His future blessings, reminding them during their most skeptical periods of His ongoing promise to grant them descendants who would inherit the Promised Land. Jews, Arabs, and Christians all trace their ancestry back to this era of human history. Abram becomes the father of the Jews, and Ishmael the father of the Arabs. Christians view themselves as Abram's spiritual heirs.

However, only Christians truly understand how these chapters uphold faith and trust in God as the channel through which God fulfills His promises. In the words of Genesis 15:6: "Abram believed the LORD and He credited it to him as righteousness." This is the same principle used by God to bring Christians to salvation. We believe God's promise that Jesus died on the cross for our sins so we can enjoy eternal life. God credits our faith in this promise as righteousness. We who were separated from God by sin are now made right with God by grace through faith. Even as Abram and Sarai hold on to the promise of descendants who will inhabit the Promised Land, so Christians rest their faith and trust in God's salvation through Jesus' death and resurrection.

Working With the Text

God "Cuts" a Covenant (Genesis 15)

1. In Abram's time a man without children could adopt a male servant to inherit all his goods. Who was this servant according to verse 2? Nonetheless, the Lord promises to bless Abram with many descendants. What example does the Lord use in verse 5 to describe the quantity of Abram's descendants?

2. In Abram's culture when people made a covenant with one another they often slaughtered animals, and then both parties walked down an aisle with the pieces of the slaughtered animals on either side. If one of the parties failed to live up to the covenant, that party would be cursed with the same fate as the animals! Explain how God used the same method to confirm His covenant promise with Abram.

3. Notice the ominous warning Abram receives about his descendants' fate. They will be enslaved and mistreated for 400 years. But God will punish the nation that enslaves them, and they will leave that country with material wealth. Look up Exodus 1:6–13 and Exodus 12:29–36 and explain how God's promise was fulfilled.

The Consequence of Doubt (Genesis 16)

1. Abram and Sarai grew weary of trusting the Lord. Like all of us, they had their moments of weakness. In what way did Abram and Sarai violate God's will because of their lack of trust? What was the result of Hagar's pregnancy? How was she treated by Sarai and why? Describe how the "fallout" of God's promise to Abram is given to Hagar in verse 10.

2. The name Ishmael means "God hears." Why is this an appropriate name to give Hagar's son? The Arabs often point to Ishmael (and by extension, Abram) as the father of their people. If this is true, in what ways do you see the prophecy of Genesis 16:12 fulfilled today?

A Covenant of Circumcision (Genesis 17)

1. Thirteen years have passed since Ishmael's birth. Abram is now 99 years old, and Sarai is pushing 90. It seems ridiculous to think Abram could give birth by Sarai. And yet what promise does the Lord reiterate in verses 3–8? God uses a number of signs to seal His promises. One involves Abram's name change. He will be called Abraham which means "father of many." The other sign is circumcision. Who must be circumcised according to God's command? At what age? Can you think of any reason why this might be a relevant sign of God's promise rather than just a crude rite?

2. How did Abraham immediately respond to God's promise? What name was to be given to Abraham and Sarah's son? Knowing that the name Isaac means "he laughs," why is this a very appropriate name?

Three Visitors and a Plea to Spare Sodom (Genesis 18)

1. How many men appeared at Abraham's tent? Of course, they were more than just men. Who was one of them according to verse 10? Who were the other two according to Genesis 19:1? What promise does God give Abraham and Sarah? How does Sarah react to the promise? How does this response add credence to the name Isaac?

2. Describe the various ways Abraham showed hospitality to the three men. How does Jesus imitate Abraham in John 13:1–5?

It was just before the Passover Feast. Jesus knew that the time had come for Him to leave this world and go to the Father. Having loved His own who were in the world, He now showed them the full extent of His love. The evening meal was being served, and the devil had already prompted Judas Iscariot, son of Simon, to betray Jesus. Jesus knew that the Father had put all things under His power, and that He had come from God and was returning to God; so He got up from the meal, took off his outer clothing, and wrapped a towel around His waist. After that, He poured water into a basin and began to wash His disciples' feet, drying them with the towel that was wrapped around Him. (John 13:1–5)

3. The wickedness of Sodom and Gomorrah was vast. God shared with Abraham His plan to destroy the cities. God wanted to determine whether the evil was as great as He had heard. Who did He send for the discovery (verse 22)? Describe the method by which Abraham "negotiated" with God. Consider Abraham's relatives near Sodom: there was Lot and his wife, Lot's two unmarried daughters (19:8), at least two married daughters and sons-in-law of Lot(19:14), and possibly some sons (19:12). Why would Abraham want to whittle down the number of the faithful to 10?

Applying the Message

1. Let's think about the Old Testament covenant sign of circumcision for a bit. Did the eight-day-old male baby have a choice in this? Could he decide for himself whether he wanted to be in the covenant relationship or not? Who decided for him? Now read Colossians 2:11–12. How are Christians "circumcised"? Who does this "circumcising" and through what means is this done? If Baptism is the New Testament sign of being part of God's covenant in Jesus Christ, should children decide whether or not they want to be baptized? Whose responsibility is this?

> In Him you were also circumcised, in the putting off of the sinful nature, not with a circumcision done by the hands of men but with the circumcision done by Christ, having been buried with Him in baptism and raised with Him through your faith in the power of God, who raised Him from the dead. (Colossians 2:11–12)

2. Why do you think the Lord waited until Abraham was 100 years old and Sarah was 90 before He fulfilled His promise in granting them a child? What aspect of their spiritual lives did this test? Share a time when the Lord allowed your faith to be tested. Why do you think the Lord often waits before answering our prayers? And why is the relationship between Sarah and Hagar a good example of what happens when we attempt to force our will over God's?

3. After recognizing Abraham's ability to "bargain" with God about the number of righteous people in Sodom needed to spare the city, con-

sider the power of prayer. How important are the prayers of God's people? Before answering, read Proverbs 15:8, Proverbs 15:29 and Psalm 145:18–19. In what ways might this knowledge aid in your prayer life?

The LORD detests the sacrifice of the wicked, but the prayer of the upright pleases Him. (Proverbs 15:8)

The LORD is far from the wicked but He hears the prayer of the righteous. (Proverbs 15:29)

The LORD is near to all who call on Him, to all who call on Him in truth. He fulfills the desires of those who fear Him; He hears their cry and saves them. (Psalm 145:18–19)

Taking the Message Home

Review

As a means of reviewing Genesis 15–18, spend some time meditating on what God has demonstrated through these chapters. Write down those areas of your life where you are finding it difficult to trust the Lord. After listing those areas, write down the prayers you would like to offer for each area of weakness. Then pray them to the Lord.

Looking Ahead

Read Hebrews 11:17–19. The author reminds us Abraham was willing to sacrifice his one and only son believing the Lord would still remain true to His promise. The Lord in His great mercy stopped Abraham just before the sacrifice. In contrast, the Lord allowed His one and only Son Jesus to sacrifice His life on the cross for our sins. Reflect on the depth of love toward us demonstrated by this act.

Working Ahead

Select one or more of the following activities to complete before the next session:

1. Examine the map from the last session and determine where Sodom and Gomorrah may have existed. Then try to find a more detailed map of this area in a Bible atlas. What is the name of the sea by which Sodom and Gomorrah probably rested?

2. Spend some time contemplating what area of your life would be most difficult to sacrifice. Would it be your house? Your money? Your spouse? Your children? What would be your reaction if God asked you to relinquish those blessings?

Did You Know That ... ?

God has various names in Genesis. In Genesis 1 the Hebrew word for God is *elohim*. This is the plural word for *God,* but it is used with a singular verb suggesting the profound mystery of the Trinity, that is, the existence of three persons in one God.

In other sections of Genesis the name for God is Yahweh. Whenever *Lord* is capitalized LORD in the New International Version of the Bible, it is refering to this name. Yahweh literally means "He causes to be" or "He brings into existence." What an appropriate name for the Creator of the universe! The name is altered just a bit when God appears to Moses in the burning bush (Exodus 3:14). He calls Himself "I AM WHO I AM." When Jesus is arrested in the Garden of Gethsemane, He refers to Himself as the "I am" three different times (John 18:5, 6, 8). By identifying Himself in this fashion, He links Himself to the Trinity.

By the third century B.C., the Jews, out of reverence for God's holy name, refused to pronounce the name Yahweh. Instead, they substituted the word *adonai* which simply means "lord." Later, the vowels of the word *adonai* were placed next to the consonants of *Yahweh,* which some Christians then mistakenly read as "Jehovah."

In Genesis 17:2 God also calls Himself "God Almighty," which, in the Hebrew, is pronounced "El Shaddai."

God commands His people not to misuse His name because these names describe who He is and what He does. So when people carelessly fling around the Lord's names, they are showing their lack of appreciation for His gracious work and will and are demonstrating a disrespect for His miraculous power and mercy.

Major Covenants in the Old Testament

COVENANTS	REFERENCE	TYPE	PARTICIPANT	DESCRIPTION
Noahic	Ge 9:8-17	Royal Grant	Made with "righteous" (6:9) Noah (and his descendants and every living thing on earth—all life that is subject to man's jurisdiction)	An unconditional divine promise never to destroy all earthly life with some natural catastrophe; the covenant "sign" being the rainbow in the storm cloud
Abrahamic A	Ge 15:9-21	Royal (land) Grant	Made with "righteous" (his faith was "credited to him as righteousness," v. 6) Abram (and his descendants, v. 16)	An unconditional divine promise to fulfill the grant of the land; a self-maledictory oath symbolically enacted it (v. 17)
Abrahamic B	Ge 17	Suzerain-vassal	Made with Abraham as patriarchal head of his household	A conditional divine pledge to be Abraham's God and the God of his descendants (cf. "As for me," v. 4; "As for you," v. 9); the condition: total consecration to the Lord as symbolized by circumcision
Sinaitic	Ex 19-24	Suzerain-vassal	Made with Israel as the descendants of Abraham, Isaac and Jacob and as the people the Lord has redeemed from bondage to an earthly power	A conditional divine pledge to be Israel's God (as her Protector and the Guarantor of her blessed destiny); the condition: Israel's total consecration to the Lord as his people (his kingdom) who live by his rule and serve his purposes in history
Phinehas	Nu 25:10-31	Royal Grant	Made with the zealous priest Phinehas	An unconditional divine promise to maintain the family of Phinehas in a "lasting priesthood" (implicitly a pledge to Israel to provide her forever with a faithful priesthood)
Davidic	2Sa 7:5-16	Royal Grant	Made with faithful King David after his devotion to God as Israel's king and the Lord's anointed vassal had come to special expression (v. 2)	An unconditional divine promise to establish and maintain the Davidic dynasty on the throne of Israel (implicitly a pledge to Israel) to provide her forever with a godly king like David and through that dynasty to do for her what he had done through David—bring her into rest in the promised land (1Ki 4:20-21; 5:3-4).
New	Jer 31:31-34	Royal Grant	Promised to rebellious Israel as she is about to be expelled from the promised land in actualization of the most severe covenant curse (Lev 26:27-39; Dt 28:36-37, 45-68)	An unconditional divine promise to unfaithful Israel to forgive her sins and establish his relationship with her on a new basis by writing his law "on their hearts"—a covenant of pure grace

Major Types of Royal Covenants/Treaties in the Ancient Near East

Royal Grant (unconditional)
A king's grant (of land or some other benefit) to a loyal servant for faithful or exceptional service. The grant was normally perpetual and unconditional, but the servant's heirs benefited from it only as they continued their father's loyalty and service. (Cf. 1Sa 8:14; 22:7; 27:6; Est 8:1.)

Parity
A covenant between equals, binding them to mutual friendship or at least to mutual respect for each other's spheres and interests. Participants called each other "brothers." (Cf. Ge 21:27; 26:31; 31:44-54; 1Ki 5:12; 15:19; 20:32-34; Am 1:9.)

Suzerain-vassal (conditional)
A covenant regulating the relationship between a great king and one of his subject kings. The great king claimed absolute right of sovereignty, demanded total loyalty and service (the vassal must "love" his suzerain) and pledged protection of the subject's realm and dynasty, conditional on the vassal's faithfulness and loyalty to him. The vassal pledged absolute loyalty to his suzerain—whatever service his suzerain demanded—and exclusive reliance on the suzerain's protection. Participants called each other "lord" and "servant" or "father" and "son." (Cf. Jos 9:6,8; Eze 17:13-18; Hos 12:1.)

Commitments made in these covenants were accompanied by self-maledictory oaths (made orally, ceremonially or both). The gods were called upon to witness the covenants and implement the curses of the oaths if the covenants were violated.

Session 6

Sodom Destroyed
and Abraham Tested

Genesis 19–22

Approaching This Study

In the book of Genesis God "cuts" a number of covenants with His people. The predominant theme in this session's readings is the fulfilling of God's covenant with Abraham through the birth of Isaac. But the fulfillment of the covenant promises are revealed in other areas as well. Abraham's nephew, Lot, is delivered from Sodom's destruction because of Abraham's covenant relationship to God. Hagar and Ishmael are protected because Ishmael is Abraham's son. The Philistine king Abimelech is cursed because he infringes on Abraham's marriage to Sarah. Notice how the covenant given Abraham affects those around him. The grace of God works in and through Abraham. He becomes a blessing to those who befriend him and a curse to those who threaten him. After all, remember the promise? "I will bless those who bless you, and whoever curses you I will curse; and all peoples on earth will be blessed through you" (Genesis 12:3).

An Overview

Unit Reading

Read chapters 19–22, perhaps with a different volunteer reading each chapter. At the end of each chapter, summarize the chapter's main theme.

The Message in Brief

Genesis 19–22 takes us from the depths of moral depravity to the soaring heights of faith. Lot, his family, and two visitors are besieged by the perverted demands of Sodom's citizenry. Lot's two visitors—who are really angels disguised as men—exhort Lot and his family to flee the city because God's judgment is imminent. Lot, his wife, and his two daughters comply, but Lot's wife is transformed into a pillar of salt when she disobeys God's command and looks back at the destruction of the city.

After being delivered from the mass destruction, Lot's two daughters seduce him into bearing their children. These children are the ancestors of the Moabite and Ammonite nations.

As Abraham continues his nomadic migration, he enters the land of the Philistines. Convinced that Sarah is Abraham's sister rather than his wife, the king of the Philistines hopes to make Sarah part of his harem until he learns of her true identity. Horrified that he has taken another man's wife, the king showers Abraham and Sarah with gifts and sends them on their way.

True to His promise, God blesses Sarah with a son named Isaac. Of course, this causes complications with Abraham's other son, Ishmael, as well as with Hagar. Upon Sarah's insistence, Abraham exiles Hagar and Ishmael, but because Ishmael is also one of Abraham's sons, the Lord protects both son and mother. One day the Lord tests Abraham's faith by commanding Abraham to sacrifice his son. Abraham follows the Lord's wishes, but the Lord stops Abraham just before the sacrifice begins and provides him with a ram to sacrifice in Isaac's place.

In stark contrast to the unbelieving hedonists of Sodom, Abraham demonstrates the divine strength that arises from faith in God's promises. Abraham's obedience to God foreshadows Jesus Christ, who allowed Himself to be sacrificed on the cross in obedience to God's will.

Working with the Text

Lot Delivered from Sodom and Gomorrah's Ruin (Genesis 19)

1. Because Lot sat at Sodom's gateway, we can imagine he had become an influential person within the community. The city gateway served as a center where judicial matters were settled. Lot may have become a judge or administrator for the city. How did Lot's hospitality toward the two angels resemble Abraham's hospitality toward the three men by his tent?

2. What were the Sodomites' intentions toward the two angels who had accompanied Lot into his house? What does this suggest about the moral depravity of the city? Lot wanted to offer his unmarried daughters to all the men of Sodom in place of the two angels. How do you react to this offer? How does this affect your opinion of Lot?

3. How many people heeded the angels' warning and fled Sodom? What did Lot's sons-in-law think of the angels' threat? What happened to Lot's wife? What does this suggest about the consequences of disobeying God?

4. How did Lot's two daughters ensure descendants? Lot fathered two different nations through his daughters. What were these two nations?

Abraham Fears Abimelech (Genesis 20)

1. After Sodom and Gomorrah's destruction, Abraham moved westward into an area bordering the Philistine territory between the cities of Gaza and Beersheba (see the map at the end of this session). The Philistines, who probably came from areas around the Aegean Sea, had recently begun settling in this area and around the coastal land of Canaan. They would become a formidable enemy in Israel's history, particularly under the reign of King Saul. So the confrontation between Abimelech and Abraham foreshadowed the rocky relationship that would exist between their descendants. Clearly, Abraham feared the king. How did he redefine his relationship with his wife Sarah? Why?

Was this a complete lie or only a half-truth? What does this suggest about Abraham's character?

2. Abraham wasn't punished for his deception. Even as the Egyptians would someday shower the people of Israel with wealth, hoping they would quickly leave, so Abimelech lavished Abraham and Sarah with wealth. Describe what Abraham gained.

Isaac Is Born (Genesis 21)

1. God's promise came true. Sarah gave birth to Isaac. Take a look at verse 6. Remembering the circumstances surrounding Isaac's name, how was Abraham and Sarah's skeptical laughter changed?

2. How did Hagar's son, Ishmael, respond to Isaac? What was God's advice in settling this problem? Again, how did God's covenant promise to Abraham "spill over" onto Ishmael?

3. Describe how the angel of the Lord protected Hagar and Ishmael because of God's love for Abraham.

4. After King Abimelech of the Philistines blessed Abraham and Sarah with great wealth, he wanted to make a treaty with them. Why? In what way did Abimelech recognize God's promise to Abraham that the nations of the world would be blessed through him?

Testing Abraham's Faith (Genesis 22)

1. God calls Isaac Abraham's "son, your only son, ... whom you love" (v. 2). Look up John 3:16 and Luke 3:21–22 and compare this to God's view of Jesus. Abraham was spared the horror of sacrificing Isaac. Was God spared the horror of sacrificing His Son? What does this say about God's love for us? Read Romans 8:31–32.

"For God so loved the world that He gave His one and only Son, that whoever believes in Him shall not perish but have eternal life." (John 3:16)

When all the people were being baptized, Jesus was baptized too. And as He was praying, heaven was opened and the Holy Spirit descended on Him in bodily form like a dove. And a voice came from heaven: "You are My Son, whom I love; with You I am well pleased." (Luke 3:21–22)

What, then, shall we say in response to this? If God is for us, who can be against us? He who did not spare His own Son, but gave Him up for us all—how will He not also, along with Him, graciously give us all things? (Romans 8:31–32)

2. How does Abraham's message to his servants (v. 5) indicate his belief in God's power to resurrect people from the dead? How does the author of Hebrews understand this (Hebrews 11:17–19)?

By faith Abraham, when God tested him, offered Isaac as a sacrifice. He who had received the promises was about to sacrifice his one and only son, even though God had said to him, "It is through Isaac that your offspring will be reckoned." Abraham reasoned that God could raise the dead, and figuratively speaking, he did receive Isaac back from death. (Hebrews 11:17–19)

3. What does Abraham believe God will provide for the sacrifice in place of Isaac (v. 8)? After reading John 1:29, 35–36 and 1 Peter 1:18–19, explain how Abraham demonstrated his role as a prophet by his statement.

The next day John saw Jesus coming toward him and said, "Look, the Lamb of God, who takes away the sin of the world!" ... The next day John was there again with two of his disciples. When he saw Jesus passing by, he said, "Look, the Lamb of God!" (John 1:29, 35–36).

For you know that it was not with perishable things such as silver or gold that you were redeemed from the empty way of life handed down to you from your forefathers, but with the precious blood of Christ, a lamb without blemish or defect. (1 Peter 1:18–19)

Applying the Message

1. Despite contemporary society's tolerance toward the homosexual lifestyle, God's Word clearly defines it as sin. Not only is it condemned in Leviticus 18:22 and 20:13, but Paul also discusses the subject in Romans 1:21–27. Read this passage carefully. According to Paul, is the

rise of homosexuality merely a rebellious act against God's will or is it also the consequence of God's judgment against society? What does this suggest about the growing influence and acceptance of the gay lifestyle in our society?

"Do not lie with a man as one lies with a woman; that is detestable." (Leviticus 18:22)

"If a man lies with a man as one lies with a woman, both of them have done what is detestable. They must be put to death; their blood will be on their own heads." (Leviticus 20:13).

For although they knew God, they neither glorified Him as God nor gave thanks to Him, but their thinking became futile and their foolish hearts were darkened. Although they claimed to be wise, they became fools and exchanged the glory of the immortal God for images made to look like mortal man and birds and animals and reptiles. Therefore God gave them over in the sinful desires of their hearts to sexual impurity for the degrading of their bodies with one another. They exchanged the truth of God for a lie, and worshiped and served created things rather than the Creator— who is forever praised. Amen.

Because of this, God gave them over to shameful lusts. Even their women exchanged natural relations for unnatural ones. In the same way the men also abandoned natural relations with women and were inflamed with lust for one another. Men committed indecent acts with other men, and received in themselves the due penalty for their perversion. (Romans 1:21–27)

2. When God created Adam and Eve, He intended one woman and one man to remain faithful to each other for a lifetime (Genesis 2:24). Throughout the Old Testament, God's people disobeyed His intent. King Solomon was one horrendous example. He possessed 700 wives and 300 concubines! Even Abraham used Hagar to beget a son. Although these individuals were great biblical heroes, they still sinned.

We are not to consider their polygamy an example for Christian living. Consider the relationship problems among Abraham, Sarah, Hagar, and Ishmael. How does their example illustrate the problems that arise when God's intent for marriage is ignored?

3. When we endure trials and tribulations we may be puzzled by the reasons for them. Can you imagine the questions that must have arisen in Abraham's mind as he took his son to the sacrificial altar? When God commanded Abraham to sacrifice his son, Abraham may not have realized it was a test of faith. Ponder the last major crisis you faced. Looking back, how might it have been a test of faith? In what way did you demonstrate faith in God's providence? Or do you feel your response manifested faithlessness? Share these insights with the others in your group.

Taking the Message Home

Review

Even as Genesis 19–22 revealed both the depths of faithlessness and moral depravity, so it displayed the paramount example of obedience and faith. Doesn't this illustrate the extremes of Christian life? There are times when our obedience and faith are strong, but soon afterward we may commit the most heinous of sins. No one is immune from these fluctuations. Read Matthew 16:13–23 and reflect on the manner in which Peter's awesome confession of faith was followed by a sin of faithlessness. Thanks be to God that Jesus' death on the cross won for us forgiveness of all sins!

Looking Ahead

The next session begins a new epoch in the Genesis account. The narrative begins to focus on Isaac and Jacob, while Sarah and Abraham face death. Spend some time reading Genesis 24 and contemplate the

Lord's role in finding a wife for Isaac. What does this suggest to you about the Lord's guidance in our daily lives?

Working Ahead

Select one or more of the following activities to complete before the next session:

1. If you are married, think back to the moment you met your spouse. What were the circumstances of your meeting? What was your immediate feeling toward the man or woman who would become your spouse? What is the one thing you remember most about his or her behavior or appearance?

2. After Sarah's death, Abraham hoped to negotiate a burial plot from the Hittites. In preparation for this story, recall the details of the last "deal" you made with a car salesman or a realtor. Did you get the best end of the deal? Why or why not?

Did You Know That ... ?

In 1924 two archaeologists by the names of W.F. Albright and M.G. Kyle found the remains of a great fortified city near the southeast corner of the Dead Sea. There were many artifacts of postherds and flints dating from a period between 2500 B.C. and 2000 B.C. There was also evidence the population abruptly ended around 2000 B.C. Because the remains show a dense population once existed, we can assume the area was very fertile. And yet, it has been desolate ever since. Something happened that changed the soil and climate. Most archaeologists believe these are the remains of Sodom and Gomorrah. Dr. M.G. Kyle states that under nearby Mt. Usdom there is a layer of salt about 150 feet thick and above it a mixture of marl (a crumbly soil made up of clay, sand, and calcium carbonate, often used as a fertilizer or in the making of cement and bricks) and sulphur, which, if ignited, would cause a great explosion. Red-hot salt and sulphur would be thrown into the sky so that it would literally rain fire and brimstone. Not only could someone be burned alive by such an explosion, but he or she could also be encrusted in salt. Interestingly, there are many pillars of salt existing today at the south end of the Dead Sea. Is one of them Lot's wife?

Session 7

The Promise Is Given to Isaac and Jacob

Genesis 23–27

Approaching This Study

Abraham never witnessed the complete fulfillment of God's promises to him. He would not see his innumerable descendants, nor would he experience their conquest of Canaan. But Abraham went to his grave trusting the future completion of God's promises. In this respect, Abraham demonstrated faith in God until his dying day. Abraham's son and grandson, Isaac and Jacob, also held fast to the promises of God. Despite their flawed characters and sinful natures, God empowered them to trust in His promises. Read the following passages about faith and discuss its nature. What is faith? What does faith give us in God's eyes? What is the object of the faith that brings eternal life?

"Now faith is being sure of what we hope for and certain of what we do not see" (Hebrews 11:1).

"This righteousness from God comes through faith in Jesus Christ to all who believe" (Romans 3:22).

"The LORD is my light and my salvation—whom shall I fear? The LORD is the stronghold of my life—of whom shall I be afraid? When evil men advance against me to devour my flesh, when my enemies and my foes attack me, they will stumble and fall. Though an army besiege me, my heart will not fear; though war break out against me, even then will I be confident. … I am still confident of this: I will see the goodness of the LORD in the land of the living. Wait for the LORD; be strong and take heart and wait for the LORD" (Psalm 27:1–3, 13–14).

"We who are Jews by birth and not 'Gentile sinners' know that a man is not justified by observing the law, but by faith in Jesus Christ. So we, too, have put our faith in Christ Jesus that we may be justified by faith in Christ and not by observing the law, because by observing the law no one will be justified" (Galatians 2:15–16).

"Jesus asked the boy's father, 'How long has he been like this?' 'From childhood,' he answered. 'It has often thrown him into fire or water to kill him. But if you can do anything, take pity on us and help us.'

" 'If you can?' said Jesus. 'Everything is possible for him who believes.' Immediately the boy's father exclaimed, 'I do believe; help me overcome my unbelief!' " (Mark 9:21–24).

An Overview

Unit Reading

This session's readings cover five chapters in Genesis. It would be worthwhile to read the chapters in their entirety. However, if time limits require the selection of only several passages, the following are recommended: Genesis 23:1–20; 24:1–32, 56–67; 25:19–34; and 27:1–46.

Genesis 27 is particularly adaptable to voice roles, including those of Jacob, Isaac, Esau, Rebekah, and a narrator.

The Message in Brief

We learned previously God gifted Abraham and Sarah with a child. But they were old, and it wasn't long before Sarah died. Because Abraham and his household lived a nomadic lifestyle, it was important for Abraham to find a permanent burial site for his wife. This session begins where Abraham successfully buries his wife in a plot of land near Mamre owned by the Hittites.

Meanwhile, Isaac grows old enough to desire a wife. Abraham is determined to find Isaac a woman from among his own people, so he sends his servant back to his old homeland. There the servant finds a beautiful and devoted wife for Isaac. Her name is Rebekah.

Rebekah gives birth to twin boys. She names the first Esau and the other Jacob. Although Jacob is the latter-born, he is determined to assume the eldest son's birthright. Even from birth Jacob attempts to "wrestle" Esau for the privilege of being firstborn. As he grows older, Jacob conspires with his mother to deceive Isaac out of Esau's birthright. Jacob receives the birthright and earns the wrath of his brother. As a result, Jacob fled flees from his family.

This session's stories paint a glorious picture of God's grace. Not only did God fulfill His promise to Abraham and Sarah, but He imparts that promise to Isaac and Jacob. As we learn about Jacob, we will discover his many faults. The fact that God chose to pass on the covenant promises to Jacob, who had some serious character defects, underscores God's mysterious grace and love. It assures us that despite our sinful and flawed nature, God will faithfully uphold His promises to us. "For it is by grace you have been saved, through faith—and this not from yourselves, it is the gift of God—not by works, so that no one can boast" (Ephesians 2:8–9).

Working with the Text

Finding a Burial Plot (Genesis 23)

1. How old was Sarah when she died? Locate the city of Hebron on the map in this session. If possible, find a modern atlas. Which country controls this city now? Who controlled the area in Abraham's day? From whom did they originate according to Genesis 10:6, 15?

2. The story of Sarah's burial plot comes alive when we remember the following about the Hittites: according to Hittite law, if a landowner sold only a portion of his property to someone, the original landowner still had to pay all the taxes on the land. Only if the landowner sold the entire property would the new owner be required to pay the taxes. What does this suggest about Abraham's intent in verses 7–9? But what did Abraham end up purchasing according to verses 17–18? What do you think of Ephron the Hittite's generosity in verses 10–11? In fact, Abraham purchased the entire property for 400 shekels (about 10 pounds) of silver—an exorbitant price. Clearly, Ephron's generosity was only superficial. He exploited Abraham's grief.

Isaac Finds a Wife (Genesis 24)

1. Abraham sent his servant back to Abraham's own country in order to find Isaac a wife. But the servant worried that any potential wife would refuse to return to Canaan. He wondered whether Isaac might leave Canaan and live with his wife back in Abraham's ancestral land. Why was Abraham adamant about Isaac living in Canaan (vv. 6–8)? What does this indicate about Abraham's ongoing faith in God's promises?

2. The servant developed a model request to screen the young women arriving at the well. What was this request? What response did the servant seek? Why would such a response suggest a woman of generous character?

3. What gifts did the servant give Rebekah? Why do you think Laban was so excited about the gifts given his sister (see v. 53 for help)? In what fashion did Rebekah's brother, Laban, demonstrate hospitality toward Abraham's servant?

Sibling Rivalry (Genesis 25)

1. Twenty years after Isaac and Rebekah were married, Rebekah gave birth to twins. What were the two boys doing when they were still in her womb? In response to Rebekah's prayers about this, God prophesied about the fate of these two sons. Paraphrase His prophecy in your own words.

2. The name *Esau* means "hairy," and the name *Jacob* means "he grasps the heel" or "he deceives." Why were these names appropriate for Rebekah's two sons? How would you describe the differences between these two sons? What role did Isaac and Rebekah play in exacerbating the sibling rivalry?

3. In the days of Abraham and Isaac, the birthright included the right to most of a father's inheritance. This was no small amount. The Ceremonial Law (Deuteronomy 21:15–17) demanded that at least a double share of the father's property would be given to the firstborn son. But the inheritance to Esau included something much more precious than a greater share of the property. What promises were being passed down from Abraham and Isaac? Would you trade such a precious promise for a bowl of stew? What does this suggest about the importance Esau placed on God's promises? How is this confirmed by the author's final remark in this chapter?

Isaac and Abimelech (Genesis 26)

How did the Lord confirm that Isaac would inherit the covenant promises given to Abraham?

Jacob Steals the Birthright (Genesis 27)

1. Rebekah suffered no misgivings about deceiving her husband into giving Jacob the birthright Esau deserved. Part of the reason for her determination was her favoritism toward Jacob. Why do you think Rebekah felt closer to Jacob than Esau? What promise had God given Rebekah when Jacob and Esau were still wrestling in her womb (Genesis 25:23)?

2. Compare the blessing Isaac gave Jacob to the one he gave Esau. What do the blessings suggest about Jacob's and Esau's descendants? Who would rule whom? Until what time? Remember, Jacob gave Esau "red stew" in exchange for Esau's birthright. And Esau was also called Edom, which means "red." Throughout most of Israel's history, the Edomites would be subservient to Israel—a sort of vassal state with kings appointed by Israel. But explain how the prophecy that "[Esau/Edom] will throw his yoke from off your [Jacob's/Israel's] neck" (v. 40) was fulfilled hundreds of years later (2 Kings 8:20–22).

In the time of Jehoram, Edom rebelled against Judah and set up its own king. So Jehoram went to Zair with all his chariots. The Edomites surrounded him and his chariot commanders, but he rose up and broke through by night; his army, however, fled back home. To this day Edom has been in rebellion against Judah. Libnah revolted at the same time. (2 Kings 8:20–22)

Applying the Message

1. The book of Genesis is a book of beginnings. Abraham began a precedent when he insisted his servant find Isaac a wife from among his own people. God would direct Abraham's descendants, the people of Israel, to avoid intermarrying with other nations or peoples. In this way they would remain a unique people of God, His "unadulterated" ambassadors to the world. Is there some merit to the argument that Christians should marry Christians and not people of other faiths? Why or why not? How does Rebekah feel about Esau's marriage to his two Hittite wives (Genesis 27:46)? What help does 2 Corinthians 6:14–16 lend to the argument?

> Do not be yoked together with unbelievers. For what do righteousness and wickedness have in common? Or what fellowship can light have with darkness? What harmony is there between Christ and Belial? What does a believer have in common with an unbeliever? What agreement is there between the temple of God and idols? For we are the temple of the living God. As God has said: "I will live with them and walk among them, and I will be their God, and they will be my people." (2 Corinthians 6:14–16)

2. Notice how Isaac duplicates his father's deception in the land of the Philistines. History repeats itself! In fact, the name of the king is still Abimelech, although this Abimelech was probably the son or grandson of the Abimelech encountered by Abraham. Do you find it alarming to see Isaac model his behavior after Abraham? Give some examples of how children can imitate their parents' behaviors.

3. Many families endure sibling rivalry. After stealing Esau's birthright, Jacob had to flee from Esau's anger and murderous intent. Twenty years would pass before they would reunite. What are some reasons you have experienced or witnessed for families dividing? How can the love God demonstrated to us "while we were still sinners" through His Son's death on the cross bring healing to families divided by anger and hatred?

4. Part of the reason for the rivalry between Jacob and Esau stemmed from their parents. Isaac favored Esau and Rebekah favored Jacob—and they didn't hide their preferences! Because of this poor parenting, Jacob experienced no guilt about deceiving his brother, and Esau sensed no guilt about his murderous intentions toward Jacob. This is one dysfunctional family! How do you feel about God's selection of Isaac and Jacob to receive His covenant promises? In what way could you find His choice very comforting?

Taking the Message Home

Review

The story of Jacob and Esau revolved around sibling rivalry. Both sons sought the favor of their parents. To review this story, think of a memory of a rivalry you endured with a brother or sister. What was it about? Why did it last? Is it still a problem in your family? What might God enable you to do to overcome it?

Looking Ahead

Jacob was certainly not the most noble individual who ever lived. But His encounters with the Lord were quite remarkable. In the next session, Jacob will not only see God and His angels traversing up and down a staircase that leads from heaven to earth, but he will also wrestle with the Lord. Write down areas of your life where you "wrestle" with God, that is, where you struggle with His will and ways.

Working Ahead

Select one or more of the following activities to complete before the next session:

1. Do you remember a book or movie in which the hero was not very likeable? It's probably difficult because we enjoy stories that have likable characters. Look up the following biblical characters and describe their shortcomings: Moses (Exodus 2:11–14), King David (2 Samuel 11:1–17), King Solomon (1 Kings 11:1–6), Peter (Matthew 26:69–75), and Saul, later named Paul (Acts 7:54–60). Why do you think it's so important that Scripture exposes the flaws of biblical heroes?

2. Read the story of Nathanael's call in John 1:43–51. Write Jesus' declaration about Nathanael found in verse 47. What did Jesus say Nathanael would see (v. 51)? Keep these two quotes handy for the next session.

3. In the next session we will read about Jacob's two wives, Leah and Rachel. The name Leah means "cow," and the name Rachel means "ewe." What is your opinion of these names? Considering how people's lifestyles in Jacob's time revolved around raising sheep and cattle, how might these names be as appropriate as contemporary names such as Amber, Lily, or Rose?

Did You Know That ... ?

Sarah was buried "in the cave in the field of Machpelah near Mamre (which is at Hebron) in the land of Canaan" (Genesis 23:19). According to Genesis 25:7–10, Abraham was buried in the same cave. Genesis 35:27–29 and 49:29–32 tell us Isaac, Rebekah, and Leah were also buried there. Genesis 50:12–13 and 50:26 indicate Jacob was the last to be buried in the cave. According to tradition, the remains of these patriarchs and their wives are located in a large cave deep beneath the Mosque of Abraham. The cave is inaccessible today, but allegedly it lies beneath the Muslim shrine in the Israeli city of Hebron.

Session 8

God Guards and Prospers His Chosen One

Genesis 28–32

Approaching This Study

Isn't God's love amazing? He loves sinners! Jacob fraudulently acquired his brother's birthright. He gained 12 sons and a daughter not through one wife, but through two wives and their maidservants. And he favored one son, Joseph, above all his other sons, thus inflaming the jealousy and anger of his other sons. The Bible reveals the weaknesses of people, including those chosen by God. This underscores the fact that God's grace is not a matter of good works, good personality, or good looks. It is His undeserved gift freely given to us. As you read these chapters, marvel at God's grace given to Jacob and to you.

An Overview

Unit Reading

Read Genesis 28–32. Due to time limits, however, the readings may be shortened to include only Genesis 28:10–22; 29:14–35; 30:25–43; 31:1–55; and 32:22–32.

The Message in Brief

The five chapters of this session's reading cover the flight of Jacob from Esau into the land of Paddan Aram. Along the way, God confirms His covenant promises with Jacob and leads him to his wife, Rachel. Jacob, the "great deceiver," is himself deceived by his father-in-law into also marrying Rachel's older sister, Leah. Great hostility arises between these two wives as they compete to bear Jacob's children. Finally, God blesses Jacob with 12 sons, including Jacob's favorite, Joseph. After working for his father-in-law for 20 years, Jacob packs his family and possessions and returns to Canaan. He must return because God had promised the land of Canaan to Jacob's descendants.

Working with the Text

A Stairway from Heaven (Genesis 28:10–22)

1. Isaac and Rebekah were disgusted with Esau's Hittite wives. They didn't want Jacob to marry a Canaanite. So they directed Jacob back to his grandfather's land in northwest Mesopotamia to find a wife from among his cousins. Only after Isaac and Rebekah's command to Jacob did Esau realize how displeased his parents were with his Hittite wives. So, in an attempt to appease his parents, Esau married a third wife, a cousin, the daughter of Ishmael. Meanwhile, Jacob headed for the homeland of his relatives. Describe Jacob's dream. Who was ascending and descending on the ladder or stairway? Who stood at the top? How does the Lord describe Himself? Can you decipher from His description a support for the promise of eternal life? How does God reiterate His covenant promise with Jacob?

2. What did Jacob call the place in which he had his dream? Look up the name in a Bible dictionary. What does the name mean? How did Jacob promise to respond to God's promises?

3. Read the story of Nathanael's call in John 1:43–51. Consider these facts: the name *Jacob* means "deceiver." Jacob's name would soon be changed to Israel. When Jesus first met Nathanael, how did Jesus describe him? How does Nathanael differ from the original "Israel"? What great reality only dreamt about by Jacob will Nathanael see? What could Jesus be referring to? Read 1 Timothy 2:5 and Ephesians 2:14–16.

The next day Jesus decided to leave for Galilee. Finding Philip, He said to him, "Follow Me." Philip, like Andrew and Peter, was from the town of Bethsaida. Philip found Nathanael and told him, "We have found the one Moses wrote about in the Law, and about whom the prophets also wrote—Jesus of Nazareth, the son of Joseph." "Nazareth! Can anything good come from there?" Nathanael asked. "Come and see," said Philip. When Jesus saw Nathanael approaching, He said of him, "Here is a true Israelite, in whom there is nothing false." "How do you know me?" Nathanael asked. Jesus answered, "I saw you while you were still under the fig tree before Philip called you." Then Nathanael declared, "Rabbi, You are the Son of God; You are the King of Israel." Jesus said, "You believe because I told you I saw you under the fig tree. You shall see greater things than that." He then added, "I tell you the truth, you shall see heaven open, and the angels of God ascending and descending on the Son of Man." (John 1:43–51).

For there is one God and one mediator between God and men, the man Christ Jesus. (1 Timothy 2:5)

For He Himself is our peace, who has made the two one and has destroyed the barrier, the dividing wall of hostility, by abolishing in His flesh the law with its commandments and regulations. His purpose was to create in Himself one new man out of the two, thus making peace, and in this one body to reconcile both of them to God through the cross, by which He put to death their hostility. (Ephesians 2:14–16)

Jacob Marries Two Sisters (Genesis 29:14–35)

1. When Jacob reached his relatives' homeland, he saw sheep about to be watered at a well. A stone covered the well. One of Jacob's cousins, Rachel, who was a shepherdess, approached the well. She was very beautiful. Jacob immediately fell in love with her. He moved the stone and uncovered the well for Rachel, then kissed her. Jacob was determined to marry her. How long did Jacob promise to work for Laban in order to wed Laban's daughter, Rachel? How long did these years seem to Jacob? What an expression of love!

2. How did Laban deceive Jacob, "the deceiver"? What would Jacob have to do in order to marry Rachel as well as Leah? So, how many years did Jacob ultimately work in order to receive Rachel? How long did you court or date your spouse before marriage?

3. Even though Jacob much preferred Rachel, Leah gave birth to Jacob's first four sons. Name them. Even though Leah was slighted by Jacob, the Lord richly blessed her. One of her sons was Levi. What would become of the tribe of Levi according to Numbers 3:5–10? Leah's fourth son was Judah. What was Jacob's promise about Judah's descendants in Genesis 49:10? How was this fulfilled in 2 Samuel 2:4 and Matthew 1:3, 16?

> The LORD said to Moses, "Bring the tribe of Levi and present them to Aaron the priest to assist him. They are to perform duties for him and for the whole community at the Tent of Meeting by doing the work of the tabernacle. They are to take care of all the furnishings of the Tent of Meeting, fulfilling the obligations of the Israelites by doing the work of the tabernacle. Give the Levites to Aaron and his sons; they are the Israelites who are to be given wholly to him. Appoint Aaron and his sons to serve as priests; anyone else who approaches the sanctuary must be put to death." (Numbers 3:5–10)

> Then the men of Judah came to Hebron and there they anointed David king over the house of Judah. (2 Samuel 2:4)

> Judah the father of Perez and Zerah, whose mother was Tamar, … and Jacob the father of Joseph, the husband of Mary, of whom was born Jesus, who is called Christ. (Matthew 1:3, 16)

God Prospers Jacob (Genesis 30:25–43)

Rachel grew jealous of Leah's ability to bear children. Rachel could not. So she chose her maidservant Bilhah to give birth to Jacob's children for her! The cycle of jealousy escalated when Leah began competing with Rachel for children. Leah gave her maidservant to Jacob so she could bear children for Jacob as well. So Jacob's 5th, 6th, 7th, and 8th sons were born through his wives' maidservants. Leah was able to give birth to two more sons, Jacob's 9th and 10th. Finally, Rachel herself became pregnant and gave birth to Joseph. Joseph was Jacob's favorite son; he is the central character of the next great epoch we study in Genesis. Between all these sons, only one daughter, born to Leah, is mentioned. Her name is Dinah. Perhaps there were other daughters not recorded in Scripture, but Dinah is an important figure in an upcoming chapter. As Jacob continued working for his father-in-law, Laban, he was accompanied by two wives, two concubines, and 11 sons. With all those dependents, it was important for Jacob to prosper! Focus on verses 31–43 and explain how Jacob engineered his prosperity.

The Pursuit (Genesis 31)

1. Jacob began to feel unwanted by Laban's family. Why? Where did the Lord command Jacob to go? Consider Laban's reaction to Jacob's flight. Although he chased Jacob and his entourage, Laban was commanded by God not to say anything to Jacob when meeting him. But Laban did express his feelings to Jacob. How do you think those expressions made Jacob feel? Describe how Jacob and Laban made peace with one another.

2. What did Rachel do with her father's household gods? It might seem puzzling to contemplate why Jacob's wife should be so fond of pagan gods. Recent archaeological discoveries have suggested that in Jacob's day, those who possessed the household gods were entitled to receive the family inheritance. How does this help explain Rachel's motives for her actions? Is this supported by Rachel's and Leah's complaint in verses 14–15?

Jacob Wrestles with God (Genesis 32:23–32)

As Jacob returned to Canaan, Esau was ready for a confrontation. Esau had some business to settle with his deceitful brother. However, Jacob showered Esau with gifts, hoping to pacify Esau with the bounty: goats, ewes, rams, camels, cows, bulls, and donkeys. Then Jacob sent his entire household ahead of him into Esau's land. Jacob stayed behind. A man appeared and wrestled with Jacob all night. Who was this figure? What did the figure do with Jacob's name? Look up Jacob's new name in a Bible dictionary and write its meaning. What other characters have we studied whose names were changed?

Applying the Message

1. Do you believe in "love at first sight?" Why or why not? Even though Jacob's love for Rachel seemed to bloom instantly, their marriage was delayed seven years during which time Jacob worked for her hand. How long do you think a couple should be engaged before marriage? Why?

2. Take a look at the "Genealogy from Terah to the Israelites." Notice

how Genesis explains the origin not only of the Israelites, but also the Arameans, Moabites, Ammonites, and Edomites. These will become important nations in the history of God's people. Look up the nations of Ammon, Edom, Moab, and Aram on the map at the end of this session. How will these people someday reside near the 12 tribes of Israel? Next, look at the diagram of "The 12 Sons of Israel" and locate on the map where the descendants of each of Jacob's sons finally resided. How do we as Christians sometimes feel that we are surrounded by pagans? How does this provide us a unique opportunity to witness about our faith in Jesus who willingly suffered and died on the cross to win salvation for all people?

3. God manifested His love for Jacob in the form of prosperity. This was also true of Abraham and Isaac. Do you think God always demonstrates His love for His chosen in the form of material wealth? Consider the apostle Paul, specially chosen by Jesus to be His apostle to the world. Read 2 Corinthians 11:22–29 and list the many sufferings Paul endured because God chose him. Share other examples of strong believers in Christ who have suffered.

Are they Hebrews? So am I. Are they Israelites? So am I. Are they Abraham's descendants? So am I? Are they servants of Christ? (I am out of my mind to talk like this.) I am more. I have worked much harder, been in prison more frequently, been flogged more severely, and been exposed to death again and again. Five times I received from the Jews the forty lashes minus one. Three times I was beaten with rods, once I was stoned, three times I was shipwrecked, I spent a night and a day in the open sea. I have been constantly on the move. I have been in danger from rivers, in danger from bandits, in danger from my own countrymen, in danger from Gentiles; in danger in the city, in danger in the country, in danger at sea; and in danger from false brothers. I have labored and toiled and have often gone without sleep; I have known hunger and thirst and have often gone without food; I have been cold and naked. Besides everything else, I face daily the pressure of my concern for all the churches. Who is weak, and I do not feel weak? Who is led into sin, and I do not inwardly burn? (2 Corinthians 11:22–29)

4. Like Jacob, when or how have you "wrestled" with God? Describe the circumstances. Notice that when God wrestled with Jacob, He let Jacob win. Do you think it's fair to say we often must wrestle with God before He lets us succeed? Why do you think He does that?

Taking the Message Home

Review

Reflect on the difficulties of polygamy as demonstrated by Jacob's wives. God's commandment "You shall not commit adultery," like all of His moral laws, is meant to keep us from offending God and harming each other. Describe how God's Law can be a helpful gift.

Looking Ahead

If time permits, scan Genesis 33–36. Be ready to share with others the most surprising elements of your reading.

Working Ahead

Select one or more of the following activities to complete before the next session:

1. After working for 20 years for Laban, Jacob returned to Canaan and reconciled with his brother Esau. In preparation for the warm story of their reunion, think of someone you have not spoken to for a long period of time. Try to get in touch with that individual before the next session.

2. Two of Jacob's sons will wreak havoc on a Canaanite family because one of them violates their sister, Dinah. Rather than allow an intermarriage between Dinah and a Canaanite, Reuben and Levi destroy the Canaanites. Their destruction becomes a model for the "separateness"

of God's people from the Canaanites. Do you think Christians should separate themselves from the rest of the world? Why or why not? What do Matthew 28:18–20; Mark 16:15; and Acts 1:7–8 suggest?

Did You Know That ... ?

The promise given Abraham that his descendants would possess the land of Canaan was fulfilled in the time of Joshua. The record of Canaan's conquest is found in the biblical book named after this leader. When the Israelites conquered Canaan, they distributed portions of the land to each of the 12 tribes of Israel. The tribes became united under the reigns of King Saul, King David, and King Solomon. After King Solomon's death, the northern tribes rebelled against the southern tribe of Judah. The Northern Kingdom anointed their own king and called their united peoples Israel. The southern tribe was ruled by a separate king and called itself Judah. The Northern Kingdom of Israel was finally conquered by the Assyrians in 722 B.C. The Southern Kingdom of Judah was destroyed by the Babylonians in 586 B.C. There would not be another nation called Israel until after the Second World War.

The Genealogy from Terah to the Israelites

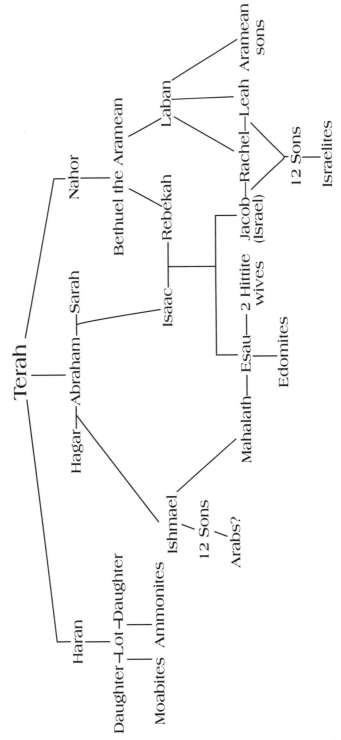

The 12 Sons of Israel

Leah——Jacob——Rachel

(Zilpah)   (Bilhah)

(7) Gad   (1) Reuben   (11) Joseph   (5) Dan

(8) Asher   (2) Simeon   (12) Benjamin   (6) Naphtali

(3) Levi

(4) Judah

(9) Issachar

(10) Zebulun

From these 12 sons would arise the 12 tribes of Israel.

Session 9

The End of an Era

Genesis 33–36

Approaching This Study

As we have seen, Genesis is easily divided into periods that focus on different biblical characters. The first great period revolves around Adam and Eve, the second around Noah, the third around Abraham, and the fourth around Isaac and Jacob. This session's chapters tie up some loose ends concerning Jacob and his brother Esau, laying the groundwork for the next and last great section of Genesis, which will focus on Jacob's favorite son, Joseph. Remarkably, the promises of God pass from one generation to another. Within each generation, the grace and blessings of the Lord focus on certain individuals chosen by God. After Adam and Eve, Seth was chosen over Cain. Of all the peoples of the world, Noah was gifted with God's favor, and of Noah's sons, Shem was favored by God. Abraham was selected over his brothers Nahor and Haran. Jacob was given the birthright rather than Esau. In the same way, God graciously blessed Joseph and worked through him to form the beginning of Israel's sojourn to Egypt. To us, God's choices may seem mysterious and arbitrary, but we rest our faith on the conviction that His ways are best for His people and kingdom.

An Overview

Unit Reading

These four chapters are rather short and should be read in their entirety with the exception of Genesis 36. Because most of chapter 36 is a list of Esau's descendants, only the first eight verses need be read if time is short.

The Message in Brief

What a wondrous thing to see Jacob and Esau reconciled! Jacob greets Esau with fear, but to his amazement, experiences his brother's grace and forgiveness. Reconciliation does not end all vestiges of sin in the world. Jacob's daughter is violated by a Hivite man, and in revenge, her brothers treacherously design the destruction of the Hivites and their village. God commands Jacob to return to Bethel, the scene of his life-changing dream, where God reaffirms His promises to Israel. God strengthens Jacob, enabling him to endure his wife's death in childbirth and his father's death by old age. Although Jacob lives in the Promised Land, his brother, Esau, moves toward the hills of Seir, which will later become the kingdom of Edom.

Working with the Text

Jacob and Esau Reunite (Genesis 33)

1. Twenty years had passed since Jacob and Esau had seen each other. Remember, after stealing Esau's birthright, Jacob had fled in terror from Esau's threats. There were no telephones or E-mail for either of them to use to correspond with each other. They did not communicate with each other for 20 years. What fears do you think Jacob experienced as he watched Esau thunder toward him with 400 men? How did Jacob's arrangement of his maidservants, wives, and children exhibit his fears?

2. Esau's reaction to Jacob was surprising. Instead of annihilating Jacob and his family, how did Esau respond? Read Luke 15:11–20 and ponder the parable of the prodigal son. Compare Esau's response to the father's action in this parable. The parable of the prodigal son pictures the relationship between sinners and God. How would you characterize God's love for His people even though they sin against Him? How does Esau's response toward Jacob model God's grace toward His children? (Look especially at Genesis 33:10.)

Jesus continued: "There was a man who had two sons. The younger one said to his father, 'Father, give me my share of the estate.' So he divided his property between them. Not long after that, the younger son got together all he had, set off for a distant country and there squandered his wealth in wild living. After he had spent everything, there was a severe famine in that whole country, and he began to be in need. So he went and hired himself out to a citizen of that country, who sent him to his fields to feed pigs. He longed to fill his stomach with the pods that the pigs were eating, but no one gave him anything. When he came to his senses, he said, 'How many of my father's hired men have food to spare, and here I am starving to death! I will set out and go back to my father and say to him: Father, I have sinned against heaven and against you. I am no longer worthy to be called your son; make me like one of your hired men.' So he got up and went to his father. But while he was still a long way off, his father saw him and was filled with compassion for him; he ran to his son, threw his arms around him and kissed him." (Luke 15:11–20)

3. When Jacob fled from Esau he took only his staff. Twenty years later he returned wealthy. He possessed two wives and their maidservants, 11 sons and one daughter, plus innumerable sheep and cattle. He wanted to give Esau a portion of his riches as a token of friendship and submission. What was Esau's reaction to Jacob's gift? After Jacob had fled from Esau, he had envisioned a stairway between heaven and earth upon which angels ascended and descended. He had been so awed by the dream that he had made a vow (28:20–22). After 20 years of exile in which he experienced God protection and guidance, how did Jacob demonstrate his appreciation for God's providential care?

The Sordid Saga of Dinah (Genesis 34)

1. We are aware of only one daughter born to Jacob's two wives and two maidservants. Her name was Dinah, and she was borne by Leah

(Genesis 30:21). The record of Dinah's birth is important because of the story found in this chapter. Shechem violated Dinah. Jacob had bought a piece of land from Shechem and his brothers to praise God for his safe return to Canaan (33:19–20). Shechem was a Hivite. Who was the father of the Hivites according to Genesis 10:15–18? Not only did Shechem want to marry Dinah, but what did his father suggest about all of Jacob's descendants and the Canaanite sons and daughters? Why was this an atrocious idea according to Deuteronomy 7:3–4? How does the Canaanite suggestion relate to the horrific sin that had resulted in the flood (Genesis 6:1–2)?

> Do not intermarry with them. Do not give your daughters to their sons or take their daughters for your sons, for they will turn your sons away from following Me to serve other gods, and the Lord's anger will burn against you and will quickly destroy you. (Deuteronomy 7:3–4)

2. What motivated the Canaanites to suggest intermarriage between Jacob's sons and their daughters (Genesis 34:20–23)? Jacob's sons deceitfully agreed to the Hivite terms provided the Hivites were circumcised. Describe the defeat of the Hivites. Which sons were instrumental in destroying the Hivite city? How were these sons related to Dinah according to Genesis 29:33–34 and 30:21? What happened to the men in the Hivite city? What about their possessions?

3. The destruction of the Hivite city is an important precedent for the actions of Jacob's descendants. Many centuries later, after the people of Israel were freed from Egyptian slavery and had wandered for 40 years in the wilderness, Joshua led the Israelites across the Jordan and back into the land of Canaan. According to God's promise, they would inhabit the land. But since the land was already occupied, the Israelites were given the right to destroy its pagan inhabitants. Read Joshua 6:24 and 8:1–2. How does the reality of Canaan's destruction suggest to you that

God is not only merciful, but also just? How does this justice manifest itself on Judgment Day (Matthew 25:31–46)?

> Then they burned the whole city and everything in it, but they put the silver and gold and the articles of bronze and iron into the treasury of the LORD's house. (Joshua 6:24)

> Then the LORD said to Joshua, "Do not be afraid; do not be discouraged. Take the whole army with you, and go up and attack Ai. For I have delivered into your hands the king of Ai, his people, his city and his land. You shall do to Ai and its king as you did to Jericho and its king, except that you may carry off their plunder and livestock for yourselves. Set an ambush behind the city." (Joshua 8:1–2)

The Deaths of Rachel and Isaac (Genesis 35–36:8)

1. Jacob's beloved wife, Rachel, died giving birth to Jacob's 12th son, Benjamin. She was buried near Ephrah, a town that would one day be known as Bethlehem. Bethlehem has always been a small village near Jerusalem. Even though its size has never been remarkable, some remarkable things have happened there. For example, read Ruth 1:1–2. Where does Naomi come from? Naomi was the mother-in-law of Ruth, who is the central character in the book of Ruth. Now read Matthew 1:5–6. How was Ruth related to King David and King Solomon? Now turn to 1 Samuel 16:4, 13. Who else came from Bethlehem? Finally, read Luke 2:1–7 and discover the other notable birth in Bethlehem. Not bad for a tiny village!

> In the days when the judges ruled, there was a famine in the land, and a man from Bethlehem in Judah, together with his wife and two sons, went to live for a while in the country of Moab. The man's name was Elimelech, his wife's name Naomi, and the names of his two sons were Mahlon and Kilion. They were Ephrathites from Bethlehem, Judah. And they went to Moab and lived there. (Ruth 1:1–2)

Salmon the father of Boaz, whose mother was Rahab, Boaz the father of Obed, whose mother was Ruth, Obed the father of Jesse, and Jesse the father of King David. David was the father of Solomon, whose mother had been Uriah's wife. (Matthew 1:5–6)

Samuel did what the LORD said. When he arrived at Bethlehem, the elders of the town trembled when they met him. They asked, "Do you come in peace?" … So Samuel took the horn of oil and anointed him in the presence of his brothers, and from that day on the Spirit of the LORD came upon David in power. Samuel then went to Ramah. (1 Samuel 16:4, 13)

In those days Caesar Augustus issued a decree that a census should be taken of the entire Roman world. (This was the first census that took place while Quirinius was governor of Syria.) And everyone went to his own town to register. So Joseph also went up from the town of Nazareth in Galilee to Judea, to Bethlehem the town of David, because he belonged to the house and line of David. He went there to register with Mary, who was pledged to be married to him and was expecting a child. While they were there, the time came for the baby to be born, and she gave birth to her firstborn, a son. She wrapped him in cloths and placed him in a manger, because there was no room for them in the inn. (Luke 2:1–7)

2. Remember how the firstborn son was entitled to be blessed with most of his father's inheritance? Reuben was Jacob's firstborn son. But how did he take sinful advantage of his favored position (35:22)? Reuben began acquiring Jacob's "possession" before Jacob's death. This was both insolent and premature. As a result, what happened to his rights as the firstborn son (1 Chronicles 5:1–2)?

The sons of Reuben the firstborn of Israel (he was the firstborn, but when he defiled his father's marriage bed, his rights as firstborn were given to the sons of Joseph son of Israel; so he could not be listed in the genealogical record in accordance with his birthright, and though Judah was the strongest of his brothers and a ruler came from him, the rights of the firstborn belonged to Joseph. (1 Chronicles 5:1–2)

3. After Jacob had envisioned a staircase connecting heaven and earth, he had named the place Bethel. Where did God command Jacob to return in Genesis 35:1? How did Jacob wish to purify his household before they reached Bethel? Describe the promises given Jacob again at Bethel and the confirmation of Jacob's new name.

4. Both Esau and Jacob prospered, but their mutual prosperity was accompanied by a problem. What difficulty did Esau and Jacob face living so close to each other? How was the problem solved? Notice, Jacob remained in the land of Canaan. How would this arrangement work to fulfill God's gift of the Promised Land?   .

Applying the Message

1. Have you ever been involved in a feud with a family member or relative? If you feel comfortable talking about it, share the experience with others in your group. What happened to instigate the family division? How long has it been going on? Has it been resolved? How? If not, how might it be resolved? How do Jesus' words in Matthew 5:23–24 relate to your situation?

"Therefore, if you are offering your gift at the altar and there remember that your brother has something against you, leave your gift there in front of the altar. First go and be reconciled to your brother; then come and offer your gift." (Matthew 5:23–24)

2. Jacob experienced the death of his beloved wife, Rachel, and the death of his father, Isaac, within a relatively short period of time. It is a sad fact that we can lose a number of loved ones within a short time period. Some people experience an extraordinary number of personal losses—financial setbacks, divorce, physical illnesses—in an ongoing series of events. If you have endured a particularly devastating series of losses, describe the feelings that you have experienced. Is there a growing skepticism about the Lord's guidance and protection? Is it difficult to face the future with confidence and assurance in the Lord's providential care? Or has it been an opportunity to discover a more durable faith in Christ Jesus?

3. Violence against women is nothing new. As we saw in this session, Dinah faced violence. Certainly, Lot's daughters experienced it. What does it mean to witness the same sinful violence among people from in the distant past? How does this suggest humans will never overcome the basic problem of sin on their own? What does this suggest about a need for a Savior? How does this underscore the importance of Jesus' ministry?

Taking the Message Home

Review

Ponder some of the themes evident in this session's chapters that are repeated throughout the Old Testament: the Promised Land; the many descendants promised to Abraham; circumcision as a sign of the covenant between God and His people; and Israel's role as a people separated from the nations of the world. Do you see the many ways in which Genesis stands as the "beginning" of our understanding of Scripture?

Looking Ahead

If time permits, read Genesis 37–41. Notice how the focus of the Genesis account now turns to Jacob's son, Joseph. Try to gain an understanding of Joseph's personality. What were his strengths? What might have been a weakness?

Working Ahead

Select one or more of the following activities to complete before the next session:

1. Joseph's dreams will be central to the next few chapters of Genesis. What role do you think dreams play in people's lives? Are they simply a hodgepodge of disjointed ideas and images? Do they access the mind's subconscious? Do you think dreams ever foretell the future? Be ready to share your opinions with others in your group.

2. Another aspect of Joseph's life is sexual temptation. Read the story of his encounter with Potiphar's wife in Genesis 39, and consider how Joseph's behavior might differ from the behavior of a young man in a sexually "liberated" culture such as our own.

3. Joseph was Jacob's favorite son, and Jacob was hardly discrete in demonstrating his favoritism. In Genesis, notice how each generation seems determined to play favorites with their children. And the results are always destructive. Why does this behavior continue from generation to generation? Why doesn't someone stop it? Do you think it's fairly common for a dysfunctional family system to continue from generation to generation? Think of some examples to share with others, without divulging names or confidences, during the next session.

Did You Know That ... ?

The word *El* is a Hebrew word for God. Many names in Hebrew end with the syllable el, for example, Daniel, Ezekiel, Nathanael, Michael, Joel, and Israel. Whenever we read a Hebrew name with such an ending, we know the name describes some quality about the Lord for which the individual has been named.

Daniel means "God is my judge"; Ezekiel means "the strength of God"; Nathanael means "God has given"; Michael means "who is like God?"; Joel means "the Lord is God"; and Israel means "he struggles with God."

Places can also carry this suffix. Jacob named the place where he wrestled with God Peniel, which means "the face of God." The Hebrew word *beth* means "house." So, when Jacob named the place of his dream, he called it Bethel, which means "house of God."

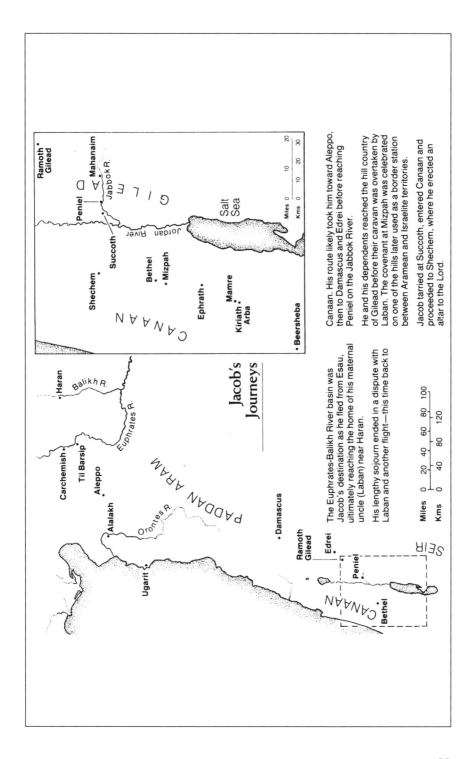

Jacob's Journeys

The Euphrates-Balikh River basin was Jacob's destination as he fled from Esau, ultimately reaching the home of his maternal uncle (Laban) near Haran.

His lengthy sojourn ended in a dispute with Laban and another flight—this time back to Canaan. His route likely took him toward Aleppo, then to Damascus and Edrei before reaching Peniel on the Jabbok River.

He and his dependents reached the hill country of Gilead before their caravan was overtaken by Laban. The covenant at Mizpah was celebrated on one of the hills later used as a border station between Aramean and Israelite territories.

Jacob tarried at Succoth, entered Canaan and proceeded to Shechem, where he erected an altar to the Lord.

Session 10

Joseph's Prophetic Dreams

Genesis 37–41

Approaching This Study

Genesis 37 marks the beginning of the fifth and final epoch in this "book of beginnings." The story focuses primarily on Jacob's favorite son, Joseph. His remarkable life story is as exciting as the greatest of adventure novels. Although his brothers attempt to rid him from their lives, the Lord chooses Joseph to be the recipient of His grace and mercy. As a result of his chosen status, Joseph suffers. But God protects and provides for His special child through a series of events that lead Joseph to acquire great power and wealth in Egypt. Joseph provides not only a model for the people of Israel who will suffer in Egypt before God rescues them, but also a foreshadowing of the humiliation and exaltation of Jesus Christ.

An Overview

Unit Reading

Each chapter in this session's readings is a story unto itself. After a volunteer reads a chapter, summarize the main events of that chapter before beginning the next chapter.

The Message in Brief

Joseph's 11 brothers envy and despise him. They are jealous of him because he is clearly Jacob's favorite son, illustrated by the richly ornamented robe given Joseph by Jacob. Joseph also experiences dreams that suggest all his brothers and father will one day bow down to him. This is an intolerable thought. Hoping to rid themselves of their obnoxious sibling, the brothers conspire to sell Joseph into slavery. The slave traders sell Joseph to an Egyptian named Potiphar who works as Pharaoh's captain of the guard. Potiphar's wife, whose sexual advances are rebuffed by Joseph, convinces her husband that Joseph assaulted her. As a result, Joseph is thrown into prison, where he interprets the dreams of a cupbearer and baker. When Pharaoh experiences a number of disturbing dreams, the cupbearer refers Pharaoh to Joseph. Because Joseph interprets Pharaoh's dreams and delivers the Egyptians from a deadly famine, he is given a place of high authority in the Egyptian empire. In this story of Joseph's suffering and exaltation, we marvel at the manner in which God transforms tremendous evil into bountiful blessings.

In the middle of Joseph's saga we read about Joseph's brother, Judah, who impregnates his daughter-in-law, Tamar, mistakenly believing she is a prostitute. Judah's immorality and hypocrisy are exposed when Tamar confronts Judah with her true identity. Judah's immoral behavior stands in marked contrast to the honesty and morality demonstrated by Joseph.

Working with the Text

Joseph's Big Dreams (Genesis 37)

1. Sibling rivalry can be powerfully divisive. Jacob exacerbated the rivalry by his favoritism toward Joseph. The Bible explains one reason for Joseph's favored status: Joseph "had been born to [Jacob] in his old age." But there is clearly another reason. Consider Genesis 30:1, 22–24 and explain Joseph's special importance to Jacob.

2. Jacob's brothers hated Joseph after hearing about Joseph's dreams. Describe in your own words his two dreams. How was Jacob's reaction a bit different than the reaction of Joseph's brothers? Read Luke 2:19 and notice how Mary's response to Jesus' birth resembles Jacob's response to his son's dreams.

But Mary treasured up all these things and pondered them in her heart. (Luke 2:19)

3. At Dothan, when the brothers saw Joseph approaching, what was their plan of action? How did Reuben hope to temper their murderous intent? It seems Reuben no longer had the clout over his brothers he once enjoyed. Who appears to have become the decision maker among the brothers? And what did he suggest they do with Joseph? How did the 11 brothers hope to hide their sinful deed from their father?

Judah's Incestuous Crime (Genesis 38)

1. It might seem at first glance that the story of Judah and Tamar is unrelated to Joseph's legacy. But the sordid tale plays an important role contrasting Judah's immorality and hypocrisy with Joseph's morality and honesty. Although Judah quickly succumbed to the temptation of the prostitute by the roadside, we will see in the next chapter that Joseph stood his ground against the attempted seduction by Potiphar's wife. But let's first look at Judah. Judah's initial mistake was to marry a Canaanite. What were the names of his three sons? Whom did Tamar marry first? What happened to him and why? Judah then demanded that one of his other sons, Onan, marry Tamar. Why was this necessary according to Deuteronomy 25:5–6? If Tamar gave birth to a son by Onan, whose name would that son carry? Why do you think that bothered Onan? What happened to Onan and why? Why do you think Judah was reluctant to offer his third son to Tamar?

> If brothers are living together and one of them dies without a son, his widow must not marry outside the family. Her husband's brother shall take her and marry her and fulfill the duty of a brother-in-law to her. The first son she bears shall carry on the name of the dead brother so that his name will not be blotted out from Israel. (Deuteronomy 25:5–6)

2. How did Tamar disguise herself to look like a prostitute? Did Tamar throw herself at Judah or did Judah actively seek her services?

What does this suggest about Judah's moral fortitude? What did Judah promise Tamar for her services, and what did he give her as a guarantee of payment?

3. When Judah discovered his daughter-in-law had become pregnant by engaging in prostitution, what sentence did he demand? Look up Leviticus 21:9 and notice how God's ceremonial law prescribed this judgment. Nonetheless, Judah displayed a double standard. How did Tamar confront Judah with his hypocrisy? What were the names of the twins that Tamar bore?

> " 'If a priest's daughter defiles herself by becoming a prostitute, she disgraces her father; she must be burned in the fire.' " (Leviticus 21:9)

Joseph's Sexual Temptation (Genesis 39)

1. What persuaded Potiphar to seek Joseph's management of his estate? How did Potiphar benefit from Joseph's good stewardship? Turn back to Genesis 12:3 and explain how Potiphar's good fortune was the result of God's covenant with Abram.

2. What did Potiphar's wife invite Joseph to do? How did Joseph respond? These days people often claim there is nothing wrong with adulterous behavior between two consenting adults. But what does Joseph call this activity in no uncertain terms (v. 9)?

3. Describe how Potiphar's wife framed Joseph. Even though Joseph was thrown into prison, how did the Lord continue to bless him? How was the warden blessed through Joseph?

Two Different Fortunes (Genesis 40)

Joseph continued to interpret dreams while in prison. Describe the cupbearer's dream and the baker's dream in your own words. To whom does Joseph give complete credit for his interpretations? How were these dreams fulfilled?

The Meaning of Pharaoh's Dreams (Genesis 41)

1. Describe Pharaoh's two dreams. Were the Egyptian wise men and magicians helpful in interpreting his dreams? Pharaoh learned about Joseph's ability to interpret dreams from the cupbearer. What did Joseph have to do before appearing before Pharaoh (v. 14)? What interpretation did Joseph give these dreams? How did Joseph suggest Pharaoh should respond to his prediction?

2. What items did Pharaoh give Joseph to indicate Joseph's new authority in Egypt? Read the following Bible verses and notice how these same regal adornment are similarly used to give authority to Haman, Mordecai, and Daniel: Esther 3:10; Esther 6:11; and Daniel 5:29.

So the king took his signet ring from his finger and gave it to Haman son of Hammedatha, the Agagite, the enemy of the Jews. (Esther 3:10)

So Haman got the robe and the horse. He robed Mordecai, and led him on horseback through the city streets, proclaiming before him, "This is what is done for the man the king delights to honor!" (Esther 6:11)

Then at Belshazzar's command, Daniel was clothed in purple, a gold chain was placed around his neck, and he was proclaimed the third highest ruler in the kingdom. (Daniel 5:29)

3. What were the names given Joseph's children? Look at the "Land of the Twelve Tribes" map. How would the tribe of Joseph be represented by his two children? How was the entire Egyptian nation blessed by its association with Joseph?

Applying the Message

1. Much has been speculated about the nature of dreams. Many people believe the subconscious mind can be explored through the interpretation of dreams. Others believe dreams foretell the future. Dreams should not be relied upon as an infallible source of revelation; however, in the Bible, dreams are occasionally inspired by God for the purpose of communicating with His people. How does God use dreams in the following passages?

Gideon arrived just as a man was telling a friend his dream. "I had a dream," he was saying. "A round loaf of barley bread came tumbling into the Midianite camp. It struck the tent with such force that the tent overturned and collapsed." His friend responded, "This can be nothing other than the sword of Gideon son of Joash, the Israelite. God has given the Midianites and the whole camp into his hands." (Judges 7:13–14)

The king asked Daniel (also called Belteshazzar), "Are you able to tell me what I saw in my dream and interpret it?" Daniel replied, "No wise man, enchanter, magician or diviner can explain to the king the mystery he has asked about, but there is a God in heaven who reveals mysteries. He has shown King Nebuchadnezzar what will happen in days to come. Your dream and the visions that passed through your mind as you lay on your bed are these." (Daniel 2:26–28)

But after he had considered this, an angel of the Lord appeared to him in a dream and said, "Joseph son of David, do not be afraid to take Mary home as your wife, because what is conceived in her is from the Holy Spirit." (Matthew 1:20)

And having been warned in a dream not to go back to Herod, they returned to their country by another route. When they had gone, an angel of the Lord appeared to Joseph in a dream. "Get up," he said, "take the child and His mother and escape to Egypt. Stay there until I tell you, for Herod is going to search for the child to kill Him." (Matthew 2:12–13)

After Herod died, an angel of the Lord appeared in a dream to Joseph in Egypt and said, "Get up, take the child and His mother and go to the land of Israel, for those who were trying to take the child's life are dead." (Matthew 2:19–20)

While Pilate was sitting on the judge's seat, his wife sent him this message: "Don't have anything to do with that innocent man, for I have suffered a great deal today in a dream because of Him." (Matthew 27:19)

2. We admire Joseph's moral fiber and shake our heads at Judah's sinful and hypocritical behavior. Paul expressed his disgust at a situation in the Corinthian church that somewhat resembles Judah's behavior. Look up 1 Corinthians 5:1–5 and consider Paul's exhortation to the Corinthian Christians. Then read 1 Corinthians 6:15–20 and discuss why Paul believed adulterous behavior should be condemned. What does God continue to offer freely to repentant sinners? Read 1 John 1:9. What does this say about the nature of God's Law (what God desires us to do) and God's Gospel (what God has done for us in Christ Jesus)?

It is actually reported that there is sexual immorality among you, and of a kind that does not occur even among pagans: A man has his father's wife. And you are proud! Shouldn't you rather have been filled with grief and have put out of your fellowship the man who did this? Even though I am not physically present, I am with you in spirit. And I have already passed judgment on the one who did this, just as if I were present. When you are assembled in the name of our Lord Jesus and I am with you in spirit, and the power of our Lord Jesus is present, hand this man over to Satan, so that the sinful nature may be destroyed and his spirit saved on the day of the Lord. (1 Corinthians 5:1–5)

Do you not know that your bodies are members of Christ Himself? Shall I then take the members of Christ and unite them with a prostitute? Never! Do you not know that he who unites himself with a prostitute is one with her in body? For it is said, "The two will become one flesh." But he who unites himself with the Lord is one with Him in spirit. Flee from sexual immorality. All other sins a man commits are outside his body, but he who sins sexually sins against his own body. Do you not know that your body is a temple of the Holy Spirit, who is in you, whom you have received from God? You are not your own; you were bought at a price. Therefore honor God with your body. (1 Corinthians 6:15–20)

If we confess our sins, He is faithful and just and will forgive us our sins and purify us from all unrighteousness. (1 John 1:9)

Taking the Message Home

Review

As you review Joseph's amazing transformation from slave to ruler, contemplate God's work in your life. How has He kept you from harm and brought you to your current place? Knowing what He has done in the past, how can you look forward with confidence to the future?

Looking Ahead

The importance of Joseph's rise to power in Egypt becomes even more apparent in the upcoming chapters. If time permits, read Genesis 42–45 before the next session. Be ready to share with your group your impression of Joseph's cat-and-mouse game with his brothers and father.

Working Ahead

Select one or more of the following activities to complete before the next session:

1. In the upcoming chapters, Joseph's brothers will journey to Egypt, hoping to find food and nourishment in the midst of a terrible famine. When they meet Joseph, they won't recognize him and Joseph will not disclose his identity until a later date. With agreement from the study group, find a favorite disguise or costume for the next session and come prepared to guess each other's identity!

2. Be prepared to share with others the best reunion you've ever experienced. Was it a school reunion, a family reunion, or a reunion with a spouse? What were the circumstances surrounding the marvelous event? How do you feel about the memory?

3. Read Genesis 45 and notice how Joseph gives credit to God for using him to save his family from famine. How has God used each of the others in your study group to enhance His work? Make a list of the people in your group and describe their positive qualities. Then offer a prayer of thanks for their presence in your life.

Did You Know That ... ?

In the conquest of Canaan under Joshua, Judah's descendants inhabited some extensive territory that included the Hebron hill country south of Jerusalem. In time, Judah would become the dominant Israelite tribe and would produce the royal house of David. Jesus Christ Himself was born in the tribe of Judah. Despite Judah's leadership in selling Joseph to the Ishmaelites and his moral laxity in impregnating Tamar, the Lord chose one of Judah's descendants to be the Savior. What a confirmation of God's amazing grace!

Session 11

God's Plan Is Revealed

Genesis 42–45

Approaching This Study

If Jacob had been a man of integrity, he never would have tricked his brother Esau into forfeiting his birthright. If Jacob had not tricked Esau into forfeiting his birthright, Jacob would not have been forced to flee. Had Jacob not fled, he might never have been attracted to Rachel. Had he never met Rachel, he would never have been tricked into marrying Leah. If Jacob had never been tricked into marrying and having children by someone he did not love as much as Rachel, then Joseph would not have become his favorite son. If Joseph had not been Jacob's favorite son, Jacob's other sons would never have sold Joseph into slavery. If Joseph had not been sold into slavery, he would never have found his way into Pharaoh's court. And if Joseph had never been given vast authority in Pharaoh's court, he could not have delivered his family from famine. Only God has the power to transform these various and sometimes sinful links into a solid chain of events by which He can bring His people salvation!

In this session, God exhibits loving guidance over the events of His children's lives. Notice how His direction leads individuals through terribly difficult times, only to provide them a blessed and joyful end. Every one of God's children must endure sorrow and pain. We often have no clue about the purpose and possibilities of our suffering. We simply hurt. But Joseph's story reminds all those who are in the throes of crisis and tribulation that God is, and will remain, in control. In the end, God will accomplish marvelous things.

An Overview

Unit Reading

These four chapters are some of the most exciting in Scripture. They are not difficult to read or understand, and they provide a remarkable example of God's power to change evil into something positive and life-giving. The story once again lends itself to a dramatic reading. Volunteers could read the parts of the narrator, Jacob (Israel), Joseph, Reuben, Judah, Pharaoh, and all the brothers.

The Message in Brief

Genesis 42–45 provides a gripping and entertaining account of the events that sweep Jacob's sons back to their brother, Joseph. Because the famine Joseph foresaw in Pharaoh's dreams extends into the land of Canaan, Jacob and his sons suffer from a lack of food. Their only source of hope rests in Egypt. When Joseph's brothers (excluding Benjamin) arrive in Egypt, they are forced to request food from the person placed in charge of food distribution—Joseph! By doing so, they inadvertently fulfill the dreams Joseph had experienced as a young man. Rather than immediately reveal himself, Joseph threatens, bargains, and cheats his brothers to ensure the return of his blood brother, Benjamin. Then Joseph forgives his brothers, praising God's incredible power to transform that which was evil into something good. God works through the brothers' sordid actions to deliver Jacob's family from certain destruction. God's ability to recast evil into good finds its ultimate fulfillment in Jesus Christ who, though crucified and buried because of people's despicable wickedness and betrayal, is resurrected to bring forgiveness and everlasting life.

Working with the Text

The Brothers Come to Egypt (Genesis 42)

1. When Joseph's brothers arrived in Egypt and entered Joseph's presence, what did they first do (v. 6)? Relate this to Joseph's dreams in Genesis 37.

2. Joseph's brothers had not seen Joseph in 20 years. When they had committed their act of treachery against him, Joseph had only been a teenager. But now, Joseph was dressed in Egyptian clothing and was clean-shaven. Furthermore, he spoke through an interpreter. How would this allow Joseph to keep his identity hidden? How did Joseph treat his brothers? What was his goal in behaving this way?

3. Why do you think Joseph was so interested in seeing his youngest brother? On what tragic sin did Reuben blame their cold reception in Egypt? How did Reuben's lament indicate his loss of leadership in the family? Can you think of a possible reason Simeon would be held captive instead of Reuben when the other brothers returned to retrieve Benjamin?

4. Jacob's sons brought silver to Egypt with which they hoped to purchase food. When they returned, they discovered their silver had been restored to them. Why did this discovery frighten them? Why did Jacob refuse to send Benjamin to Egypt?

The Second Journey to Egypt (Genesis 43)

1. Compare Reuben's offer to Judah's offer (42:37, 43:9). Whose offer would you consider more generous and why?

2. What frightened Joseph's brothers about going to Joseph's house? What did they think would happen? But what was Joseph's intent in commanding them to come to his home?

3. When Joseph saw his younger brother, Benjamin, what did he do? Describe the seating arrangement of the meal. Who ate with whom? In what order were the brothers seated, and who received the most food?

The Big "Frame-Up" (Genesis 44)

1. Describe in your own words how Joseph framed Benjamin. What did Joseph's brothers promise would happen if Joseph's silver cup was discovered among their things?

2. When they were brought before Joseph, who spoke on behalf of all the brothers? What does this suggest about his role in the family?

3. After Joseph's cup was discovered among Benjamin's things, Judah bravely approached Joseph and begged for mercy. Summarize Judah's argument for allowing Benjamin his freedom.

The Revealing (Genesis 45)

1. After revealing himself to his brothers, how did Joseph demonstrate his emotions? How did the brothers feel about their surprising discovery?

2. What persuasive argument did Joseph use to keep his brothers from dissolving in guilt over their past actions?

3. When Pharaoh learned about Joseph's family, what command did he give them? What did he offer them to aid in their travels? What was Jacob's reaction to his sons' report?

Applying the Message

1. One of the interesting aspects of Joseph's story involves the economic principle that gave him such power. Joseph planned ahead and saved resources during times of plenty to be used during periods of drought. This principle enables people to weather difficult times even today. How easy is it to save for the "rainy day"? Those of you who have saved successfully, share the principles by which you have operated. What challenges have you experienced and how have you overcome them?

2. For many people, it is important not to cry during times of emotional turmoil. But consider how many times we witness Joseph crying at the presence of his brothers. What does this biblical hero suggest about displaying emotions?

3. Job had more difficulties than anyone else in Scripture. Read Job 1:6–12 and explain the reason God allowed him to suffer so greatly. Job, of course, had no idea why he had been afflicted. How could he know he was the center of a cosmic contest to demonstrate the power and endurance of faith in God? Even though he had no idea of the reason for his suffering, Job continued to love and trust the Lord.

We may not know the reason for our troubles. Joseph certainly must have questioned the Lord's goodness when he was sold into slavery. In the end, God used his suffering for good. Read Romans 8:31–39. How do these words provide encouragement and comfort to you as you face suffering and hardship?

> One day the angels came to present themselves before the LORD, and Satan also came with them. The LORD said to Satan, "Where have you come from?" Satan answered the LORD, "From roaming through the earth and going back and forth in it." The LORD said to Satan, "Have you considered My servant Job? There is no one on earth like him; he is blameless and upright, a man who fears God and shuns evil." "Does Job fear God for nothing?" Satan replied. "Have You not put a hedge around him and his household and everything he has? You have blessed the work of his hands, so that his flocks and herds are spread throughout the land. But stretch out Your hand and strike everything he has, and he will surely curse You to Your face." The LORD said to Satan, "Very well, then, everything he has is in your hands, but on the man himself do not lay a finger." (Job 1:6–12)

> What, then, shall we say in response to this? If God is for us, who can be against us? He who did not spare His own Son, but gave Him up for us all—how will He not also, along with Him, graciously give us all things? Who will bring any charge against those whom God has chosen? It is God who justifies. Who is he

that condemns? Christ Jesus, who died—more than that, who was raised to life—is at the right hand of God and is also interceding for us. Who shall separate us from the love of Christ? Shall trouble or hardship or persecution or famine or nakedness or danger or sword?

As it is written: "For your sake we face death all day long; we are considered as sheep to be slaughtered." No, in all these things we are more than conquerors through Him who loved us. For I am convinced that neither death nor life, neither angels nor demons, neither the present nor the future, nor any powers, neither height nor depth, nor anything else in all creation, will be able to separate us from the love of God that is in Christ Jesus our Lord. (Romans 8:31–39)

4. When famine arose in Canaan, Jacob clearly became irritated with his sons. Consider his snide remark in Genesis 42:1. What happens when you are under pressure? In what negative way do you sometimes react? How could you channel this behavior into something more positive?

Taking the Message Home

Review

Reflect on Joseph's treatment of his brothers. Did he act appropriately toward them? Why or why not? If you were in such a situation, how would you handle the surprise of discovering your wicked brothers or sisters begging for help? What does this story suggest about friends and family who feud with one another? Meditate on these thoughts and then pray for the power to forgive others just as God in Christ forgave you.

Looking Ahead

Read Genesis 50 and list the various ways in which this chapter is an appropriate conclusion to the entire book. If you find one or two verses that highlight God's power to protect and care for His people, write the words on a piece of paper and share them with others in the group at the next session.

Working Ahead

Select one or more of the following activities to complete before the next session:

1. In the next session we read about Jacob's and Joseph's deaths. Both are concerned that their remains rest in the Promised Land. Have you considered where you will place your remains? Would you like to be buried? Where? What are your thoughts on cremation?

2. List the ways God fulfilled His promises to Adam and Eve, Noah, Abraham and Sarah, Hagar, Isaac and Rebekah, Jacob and Rachel and Leah, and Joseph. The book of Genesis is a book of beginnings. Why might it also be called a book of promises? How does the sure fulfillment of all these promises give us confidence in God's promises of forgiveness and salvation in Jesus Christ?

3. Because of Joseph's power and position in Egypt, Jacob's whole family would settle in Egypt. Read Exodus 1–2:10 and explain how Joseph's rise to power in Egypt is integral to the ongoing story of God's people, Israel, and the appearance of Moses.

Did You Know ... ?

In the end, the promises of God would not be fulfilled through Jacob's firstborn, Reuben, because he lost favor in God's eyes by sleeping with Jacob's concubine (Genesis 35:22; 1 Chronicles 5:1). Nor would they be fulfilled through the second and third sons, Simeon and Levi, because both men demonstrated their treachery in seeking revenge against the Hivites on behalf of their sister, Dinah (Genesis 34). By their sins, these three excluded themselves from receiving the fullness of God's promises. Because he was the next in line, Judah would become the spokesman for the family. His tribe would become first among all the tribes, and from his tribe would arise the Messiah, Jesus.

Joseph's brothers were unable to recognize Joseph since he was dressed and groomed as an Egyptian prince. In contrast to the Egyptian custom of being clean shaven, Hebrews wore beards.

From Lifelight Bible Study Series, *Genesis*, Part 2, Student Book (St. Louis: CPH, 1990).

Session 12

The End of the Beginning

Genesis 46–50

Approaching This Study

The final chapters of Genesis tie up some loose ends about the lives of Jacob and Joseph. Jacob moves his household to Egypt, where he and his relatives enjoy Pharaoh's generosity and protection, which Pharaoh gladly offers in gratitude for Joseph's foresight and planning. The Egyptian throne grows wealthier and more powerful through its association with Joseph, proving how God remains faithful to the covenant given Abram and his descendants: "I will bless those who bless you, and whoever curses you I will curse." The last chapters of Genesis illustrate how Joseph's legacy continues through his sons Ephraim and Manasseh. In centuries to come, the more powerful kingdom of Judah as well as Christ's eternal kingdom will arise through Judah's descendants, but the lesser Northern Kingdom of Israel will arise largely from Ephraim's and Manasseh's descendants. Upon the deaths of Jacob and Joseph, the foundation is laid for the formation of God's chosen nation of Israel. The Israelites will populate much of Egypt, but because of the Egyptians' sense of superiority, God's people will become enslaved and remain a separate entity ready to form into a united nation. God will choose Moses to solidify their national identity when He leads them out of slavery. In all ways, God demonstrates His role as the Ruler and Creator of history, moving people and events to fulfill His divine promises.

An Overview

Unit Reading

These chapters should be read in their entirety, with the exception of Genesis 46:8–25, which consists of the names of those in Jacob's house who traveled to Egypt. Although their names are interesting, they are not crucial to this session's themes.

The Message in Brief

God appears to Jacob (Israel) and encourages him to lead his family away from the Promised Land and into Egypt, promising that Israel's descendants would someday reoccupy Canaan. Jacob's 70 relatives travel to Egypt, where they are given choice land on which to live and prosper. As the famine continues in Egypt, Joseph uses its devastation to acquire greater power and wealth for Pharaoh. In this way, Joseph continues to be a blessing to those who help and befriend him. Jacob adopts Joseph's two sons, Ephraim and Manasseh, offering his greatest blessing to Ephraim. Then Jacob blesses his 12 sons, laying the foundation for the fate of the tribes that will arise from each son. Prominence is given Judah and Joseph. Jacob dies of old age and is buried in the plot of land once purchased by Abraham. After Jacob's death, Joseph assures his brothers he will continue to protect them, because God had transformed their treachery into a great blessing. Before Joseph dies, he asks to be buried in the Promised Land someday.

Many years later, after the death of great King Solomon, the nation of Israel would be divided into two. The Northern Kingdom would be called Israel, and the Southern Kingdom would be called Judah. Interestingly, the Northern Kingdom would often be called Ephraim after Joseph's son. Thus, the two kingdoms would represent Jacob's most prominent children, Judah and Joseph.

Working with the Text

Jacob Journeys to Egypt (Genesis 46:1–7, 25–34; 47:1–12)

1. The Lord appeared to Jacob in a vision at night. He brought words of comfort for Jacob's journey to Egypt. What three great promises did the Lord offer Jacob? How were these three promises fulfilled in the following passages?

> Now Joseph and all his brothers and all that generation died, but the Israelites were fruitful and multiplied greatly and became exceedingly numerous, so that the land was filled with them. (Exodus 1:6–7)

> The LORD said, "I have indeed seen the misery of my people in Egypt. I have heard them crying out because of their slave drivers,

and I am concerned about their suffering. So I have come down to rescue them from the hand of the Egyptians and to bring them up out of the land into a good and spacious land, a land flowing with milk and honey—the home of the Canaanites, Hittites, Amorites, Perizzites, Hivites and Jebusites. And now the cry of the Israelites has reached Me, and I have seen the way the Egyptians are oppressing them. So now, go. I am sending you to Pharaoh to bring My people the Israelites out of Egypt." (Exodus 3:7–10)

When Jacob had finished giving instructions to his sons, he drew his feet up into the bed, breathed his last and was gathered to his people.

Joseph threw himself upon his father and wept over him and kissed him. (Genesis 49:33–50:1)

2. Genesis 46:8–25 consists of a list of Jacob's sons and grandchildren. How many people were involved in the journey, including Manasseh and Ephraim (v. 27)? How did Joseph react upon seeing his father? When Jacob approached his long lost son, how did he express his joy? Notice how the old man, Simeon, verbalized similar feelings upon seeing the Christ Child in Luke 2:25–32.

Now there was a man in Jerusalem called Simeon, who was righteous and devout. He was waiting for the consolation of Israel, and the Holy Spirit was upon him. It had been revealed to him by the Holy Spirit that he would not die before he had seen the Lord's Christ. Moved by the Spirit, he went into the temple courts. When the parents brought in the child Jesus to do for him what the custom of the Law required, Simeon took Him in his arms and praised God, saying: "Sovereign Lord, as You have promised, You now dismiss Your servant in peace. For my eyes have seen Your salvation, which You have prepared in the sight of all people, a light for revelation to the Gentiles and for glory to Your people Israel." (Luke 2:25–32)

3. How did Egyptians view shepherds? Not only did they not want to eat with the Hebrews, but they found shepherds loathsome as well! All in all, Joseph's family would not be particularly appealing to most Egyptians. What does it say about Pharaoh's feelings toward Joseph that he allowed Joseph to settle his family in "the best part of the land" (47:11)?

Joseph Handles the Famine (Genesis 47:13–31)

Clearly, Joseph's foresight concerning the famine was a boon to the Egyptian throne. When people could no longer grow their own food, they paid the Egyptian government for food. When they had no more money, how did they purchase food? How would Joseph's strategy increase the power of the throne? How did the Israelites fare in the land of Goshen? Did they suffer or prosper?

Jacob Adopts Joseph's Sons (Genesis 48)

Jacob wanted to adopt Joseph's sons. These children would take the place of the sons whom Rachel might have borne had she not died. What were the names of these two sons? Who was the oldest and justly deserved the blessing of the birthright? But to whom did Jacob offer the birthright? How did Joseph attempt to correct him? What did Jacob promise about the younger of the two brothers? Consider how Jacob achieved the birthright instead of Esau. In what way do you see history repeating itself?

Jacob Blesses His Sons (Genesis 49:1–28)

1. The blessing of Jacob is the longest poem in Genesis. Jacob's blessings would apply to the tribes that would arise from each son. Judah and Joseph were given the longest blessings. In your own words, summarize the blessings given Judah (vv. 8–10).

2. Summarize the blessings offered Joseph (vv. 22–26).

The Deaths of Jacob and Joseph (Genesis 49:29–50:26)

1. Where did Jacob wish to be buried? Why? What uniquely Egyptian practice was used to bury Jacob? Look up *embalming* in a dictionary or encyclopedia and share what such a practice involved.

2. Describe the procession that returned Jacob's body to Canaan.

3. What fear seized Jacob's brothers once their father had died? With what argument did Joseph assuage their fear?

4. When Joseph neared death, he insisted that his body be perma-

nently buried in the Promised Land. Where was he initially buried? But under what circumstances was his wish finally fulfilled (Exodus 13:17–19; Joshua 24:32)?

> When Pharaoh let the people go, God did not lead them on the road through the Philistine country, though that was shorter. For God said, "If they face war, they might change their minds and return to Egypt." So God led the people around by the desert road toward the Red Sea. The Israelites went up out of Egypt armed for battle. Moses took the bones of Joseph with him because Joseph had made the sons of Israel swear an oath. He had said, "God will surely come to your aid, and then you must carry my bones up with you from this place." (Exodus 13:17–19)

> And Joseph's bones, which the Israelites had brought up from Egypt, were buried at Shechem in the tract of land that Jacob bought for a hundred pieces of silver from the sons of Hamor, the father of Shechem. This became the inheritance of Joseph's descendants. (Joshua 24:32)

Applying the Message

1. When you consider the entire book of Genesis, you can only marvel at God's consistent guidance and protection over His people through the generations. In what way has your understanding of God changed because of your study of this book? Which of His qualities most impressed you? In the end, is this book about God's people or about God? Why?

2. One cannot read about the Egyptians' attitude toward the Hebrews and shepherds without getting a sense of their elitism. They were good at looking down at others. How is this trait still common

among people today? How does God's choices of Abraham, Jacob, and Joseph suggest the danger and absurdity of feeling superior to other people?

3. Think of the main characters found in Genesis: Adam and Eve, Noah, Abraham and Sarah, Isaac and Rebekah, Jacob and Rachel, and Joseph. If you could summarize a common theme that runs through their lives, what would it be?

Taking the Message Home

Review

As a review of many of the Genesis stories, with particular emphasis on Joseph, look up Acts 7:1–16. As Christianity gained influence in Jerusalem, the ruling Jewish religious authorities (called the Sanhedrin) grew threatened. They focused their anger on a strong believer named Stephen. Attempting to make an example of him, they brought false witnesses to accuse him of blasphemy. In response, Stephen summarized in Acts 7 how the history of Israel led to the fulfillment of God's promises in Jesus Christ.

Looking Ahead

Genesis clearly and consistently illustrates how people and nations are blessed by their association with those chosen by God. Do you think the promise given Abraham and his descendants remains with God's people today? Can you think of ways in which people and nations continue to find themselves blessed because of the influence of Christianity? What would the world be like without the Gospel message of forgiveness through faith in Christ Jesus?

Working Ahead

Select one or more of the following activities to complete during the following week:

1. In your own words summarize the covenant promises given to Abraham, Isaac, and Jacob. Write them on a piece of paper and entitle it "Old Testament Promises." Then look up Matthew 28:20; John 3:16; John 8:31–32; and Acts 2:38–39; and, on a sheet entitled "Promises to Me," record the promises given to you in these Scriptures. Keep these promises handy to lend support during difficult days. Remember that as surely as God fulfilled His promises to Abraham, Isaac, and Jacob, He will fulfill His promises to you.

2. It is admittedly difficult in this age of equal rights to ponder the secondary role endured by women in the Genesis stories. The world of Genesis was patriarchal: birthrights were assumed by sons rather than daughters, and the experiences of men were considered more significant than the life stories of women. Men were allowed to marry a number of wives who remained quite subservient to their husbands. But this was not God's original intent. Look again at Genesis 2:23 and notice the equality enjoyed by Adam and Eve before the fall. What is the cause of inequality according to Genesis 3:16? Read Galatians 3:26–28. What is God's intent for His kingdom to come?

3. Read Romans 3:23. Are there any perfect heroes in the world aside from Jesus Christ? Reflect on the manner in which Genesis emphasizes the failings found in all its characters. In what way does the Genesis account continually remind us of the need for God's grace and forgiveness?

Did You Know ... ?

Notice how Stephen stated that 75 people from the house of Jacob journeyed to Egypt (Acts 7:14). This would seem to contradict the Genesis account of 70 people. The discrepancy is the result of the different versions involved. In the Hebrew version of the Old Testament (called the Masoretic Text), the number in Genesis 46:27 is 70. In the Greek translation of the Old Testament (called the Septuagint, 285 B.C.–132 B.C.), the number is 75. Obviously, Stephen was more familiar with the Greek translation of the Old Testament than he was with the Hebrew version. There is no inherent contradiction between the Hebrew account and Stephen's speech. God's Word remains truthful and completely reliable.

Glossary

adultery. In the Old Testament, adultery refers to sexual intercourse between a man and another man's wife. Jesus interprets the Sixth Commandment as forbidding all kinds of sexual indecency in both deed and thought.

amen. The word *amen* is spoken when one wants to express "so be it." It indicates confirmation or agreement.

angels. Literally, "messengers." Unseen, spiritual, holy, heavenly beings who continually do God's bidding. Angels protect and serve those who fear God. They differ in rank and dignity.

anoint. To apply oil to a person or thing. Sometimes it was simply a part of grooming. After washing or bathing, people anointed themselves. Hosts anointed their guests as an act of courtesy or respect. Anointing was also done at a person's induction to the office of priest or king. Christ was anointed with the Holy Spirit.

Antichrist. One who is both an enemy of Christ and a usurper of His rights and names.

apocalyptic literature. This includes the books of Daniel and Revelation, which reveal events of the Last Times, judgment, and the hereafter. Apocalyptic literature uses numbers and symbols to express certain ideas.

Baptism. Christian Baptism must include the application of water in the name of the triune God—Father, Son, and Holy Spirit. The way the water is applied to the individual, however, can vary. The New Testament makes no distinction between adult and infant Baptism. Christian Baptism works the forgiveness of sins, delivers one from spiritual death and the devil, gives eternal salvation to all who believe in Christ, and offers the Holy Spirit. Baptism also makes one a member of the body of Christ, the Church.

Christ. Greek for the Hebrew word *messiah*, which means "anointed one." Jesus is the promised Messiah.

church. The collective gathering of God's people around Word and Sacraments. The New Testament speaks of the church both as some Christians gathered in a specific place and as all Christians everywhere of all time. The church is also described as the fellowship of God's people, the bride of Christ, the body of Christ, and a building of which Jesus Christ is the chief cornerstone.

circumcision. Removal of the foreskin of the penis. God instituted the rite of circumcision upon Abraham and his descendants. It showed that He would be their God, and they were to belong to Him. The Hebrew people looked down on those who were not circumcised. Controversy erupted in the early Christian church between Jewish Christians, who demanded that Gentiles be circumcised in order to be Christian, and the Gentiles, who refused. St. Paul spoke God's Word to this controversy when he declared that circumcision was not required of Gentiles who became Christians.

congregation. An assembly of people.

conversion. An act of God's grace by which a sinful person is turned around and brought into God's kingdom. Conversion is accomplished by the Holy Spirit, who brings the person to faith in Christ through the Word.

covenant. An agreement between two or more individuals, tribes, or nations, to do or to refrain from doing something.

deacon. Someone who serves. In the early church, deacons were chosen to relieve the apostles of caring for the physical needs of widows and other poor people.

demon. An evil spirit who is against God and His work. Demons are angels who rebelled against God and now follow Satan.

doctrine. Something that is taught; instruction or teaching.

Easter. Teutonic goddess of light and spring. By the eighth century the name was applied to Christ's resurrection.

elder. In the New Testament *elder* and *bishop* are used to mean the same thing: overseer. The elder or presbyter was a man the apostles appointed in each Christian congregation to be its spiritual leader.

elect. The elect are those who have faith in Christ as the promised Messiah and Savior.

election. The New Testament spells out the doctrine of election. No one deserves to be saved. God, however, desires from eternity that all people be saved. By God's grace through faith alone in Jesus, people are saved. Those who have received God's gift of faith respond in thankfulness to God for His love and grace in choosing them.

epistle. A formal letter that includes Christian doctrine and instruction.

eternal life. Eternal life begins when the Holy Spirit by grace brings a person to faith in Jesus Christ. Although the Christian already has eternal life, he or she will not experience it fully until the resurrection of the body and the life of the world to come.

faith. That belief and trust in the promise of God in Christ Jesus, worked by the Holy Spirit, through which a person is declared just, brought into a right relationship with God, and saved. The Holy Spirit works faith in Christ in the individual through the Word and the Sacraments.

fellowship. A state of sharing something in common. Christian fellowship shares the Gospel and Sacraments, faith in Christ, and various spiritual gifts. Through the work of the Holy Spirit, believers have a oneness in Christ.

forgiveness. God's act whereby He ends the separation caused by peoples' sins and puts them back into a proper relationship with Himself. Forgiveness is a gift of God, given out of grace for Christ's sake. As a result of God's forgiveness, we are to forgive our neighbor. Recognizing and being sorry for our sins precedes forgiveness.

Gentiles. Non-Hebrew nations of the world. People outside the Jewish faith.

glory. That which shows the greatness of someone or something. The glory of God is shown in and by His great miracles, His eternal perfection, His creation, and all His works. Most important, it is shown by His Son, our Lord Jesus Christ.

gnosticism. A system of belief that reached its peak in the second and third centuries. According to the gnostics, salvation came by hating the world and everything physical and by escaping to the spirit world. They said Jesus came not to save people from sin but to show them how to escape to the spiritual world.

Gospel. The Good News that God has forgiven all people because Jesus Christ has fulfilled the Law in their place and paid the penalty for their sins on the cross.

gospels. The first four books of the New Testament. Matthew, Mark, Luke, and John each wrote one of the books. They are called gospels because they tell the Good News of how salvation was won for all people by Jesus Christ.

grace. God's undeserved love and favor in Jesus Christ by which He is moved to forgive people's sins and grant them salvation. The word *grace* is sometimes used as a gift, quality, or virtue. Saving grace, however, is none of these things. It is a quality within God. It is also used to mean God's steadfast love or faithfulness.

heaven. The invisible world or universe from which God rules; the home of angels. Christ rules from heaven and receives believers there. *See also* paradise.

heir. The individual to whom another person's wealth or possessions—the person's inheritance—is given after the person dies.

hell. Either the place of eternal punishment or the punishment itself.

heresy. Stubborn error in an article of faith in opposition to Scripture.

holy. That which is set apart to be used for or by God. Holiness is the state of being without sin. The holiness of God is imparted to people through His act of choosing them in grace and through His other mighty acts. It culminates in the saving work of Jesus Christ.

hymn. A song telling about God and praising Him.

inspiration. The special way the Holy Spirit worked in certain people to cause them to act out, speak, or write God's Word. When the Holy Spirit did this, the person who was inspired was certainly under the direction of God's power (God-breathed), but he or she was not a robot.

Israel. (1) The name given to Jacob after he wrestled with an intruder (Genesis 32:28). (2) The name of the nation composed of the descendants of Jacob and his 12 sons. Jacob and his sons founded the 12 tribes of Israel. (3) The name given to the 10 northern tribes of Israel after Solomon's death, when they revolted under Rehoboam and the kingdom split in two. The Northern Kingdom was called Israel to distinguish it from the Southern Kingdom, which was called Judah. (4) All who follow in the faith of Abraham, Isaac, and Jacob and therefore are true Israelites, no matter what their physical descent.

Jesus. Greek for the Hebrew name *Joshua,* which means "savior."

Jew. Originally someone who belonged to the tribe or kingdom of Judah as opposed to those in the Northern Kingdom. *Hebrew* denotes those who descended from Abraham; *Israel* denotes those who then descended from Jacob; and *Jew* denotes those who then descended from the tribe or kingdom of Judah.

Jordan River. The most important river in Palestine. It is the river in which Jesus was baptized by John. The river is 3 to 10 feet deep and about 100 feet wide.

Judah. (1) The fourth son of Jacob and Leah. Jacob bestowed the blessing of the birthright on Judah. Jesus was one of Judah's descendants. (2) The tribe that descended from Judah. It occupied the greater part of southern Palestine. (3) The kingdom of Judah, which began when the 10 northern tribes withdrew from Rehoboam around 912 B.C. and lasted until 587 B.C., when Jerusalem fell. It existed in the southern part of Palestine.

justification. The gracious act of God by which He pronounces all people to be not guilty of their sin through faith in Jesus. The basis for His acquittal is that Jesus Christ fulfilled the Law in humanity's place and paid the penalty for all people's sin when He suffered and died on the cross.

kingdom of God. A spiritual kingdom that includes all nations. The New Testament pictures God's kingdom as the Holy Spirit in the hearts of His people. The kingdom of God is, at times, spoken of as a future blessing, as in the kingdom Jesus will bring on the Last Day, and, at times, as a present reality. The church proclaims the kingdom of God by preaching the Gospel.

Lord. (1) LORD (often printed in capital and small capital letters in the Bible) is God's personal name. It comes from the Hebrew word *Yahweh.* (2) Lord (capital *L* and the remaining letters lowercase) comes from the Hebrew word *adon.* It means "master" and denotes ownership. (3) *Adonai,* translated as Lord, is the word the Israelites said whenever they saw the consonants of Yahweh (YHWH). (4) The Greek word *kyrios* is also translated as Lord. It is the word used for a human master or for God as the ruler. It is also the word used for Christ, who by His death and resurrection is Lord.

Lord's Supper. Christ instituted this supper on the night of His betrayal to replace the Passover feast. It is a memorial for His death for the sins of the world. In this meal Christ gives His body and blood together in, with, and under the bread and wine. Christians who trust in the blessings Christ promises to give in this meal and who partake of it in faith receive the forgiveness of sins, life, and salvation along with a strengthening of their faith. Also called Breaking of Bread, Holy Communion, the Eucharist, and the Lord's Table.

love. Various types of love are referred to in the Bible. The Greek word *agape* represents God's love for sinful people. This is the kind of love Christians are to have.

mercy. God's undeserved favor and love within the covenant relationship.

Messiah. Hebrew for "anointed one." *See* Christ.

minister. A person who has been called—by God, through the church—to active service to God. All Christians have vocations—callings by God in life—and all baptized Christians have received various gifts of the Holy Spirit. All Christians are members of the priesthood of all believers (1 Peter 2:9). However, ministers have a distinct calling from God, even as Jesus chose 12 of His disciples to serve as apostles.

miracle. An event that causes wonder; something that takes place outside of the laws of nature. The New Testament depicts miracles as signs, wonders, and acts of power. Their significance could be understood only by those who had faith in Jesus Christ.

ordination. A rite (act) of the church by which the church, through a congregation, publicly confers the pastoral office on a qualified man. Ordination has its historical roots in the New Testament and in the early church. In the New Testament, deacons, missionaries, and elders were called to their offices, just as today a congregation calls a man to be its pastor.

parable. A method of speech that compares two objects for the purpose of teaching a moral or religious truth. It is an earthly story with a heavenly or spiritual meaning. The events and characters in the parable are true to nature, but not every detail of the story has a spiritual meaning. Rather there is only one main point of comparison. Jesus often spoke in parables to teach people about Himself and the kingdom of heaven.

paradise. Used in the New Testament to describe heaven, the home of those who die in Christ.

peace. Often used to describe the state of spiritual tranquility and harmony that God gives when He brings one into a right relationship with Himself.

Pentecost. The Jewish Feast of Weeks, which was celebrated 50 days after the Feast of Passover. It is also known as the Feast of Harvest and the Day of Firstfruits. On this day, the Holy Spirit was outpoured on the disciples, and many people came to faith in Christ.

prayer. Speaking with God. Prayers can be formal or spoken freely from one's own thoughts and concerns. They can be said together by a large group of believers or alone by an individual. They can be said at set times and places or at all times and places.

priest. One who represents the people before God. Through Moses, God appointed Aaron and his descendants as priests. They wore special clothing in the sanctuary, taught the people, and inquired of God's will. The chief priest, or high priest, was in charge of all the other priests. He offered the sin offering, made sacrifice on the Day of Atonement, and discovered the will of God through Urim and Thummim (sacred lots). In the New Testament, Jesus Christ is the only high priest. Since He sacrificed Himself for the sins of the people and this sacrifice need never be repeated, there is no longer a need for the Levitical priesthood. Jesus is our High Priest. The New Testament also teaches about the priesthood of all believers. Christians share in Christ's priestly activity by bringing the Gospel to people.

redemption. The buying back of humanity from sin and death by Christ, our Redeemer, who paid the price with His perfect obedience and His sacrificial death on the cross.

repentance. A total change of heart and life that God works in an individual who does not believe or trust in God by turning the individual around to, in fact, believe and trust in Him. Repentance includes both sorrow for one's sins and faith in Christ through whom forgiveness is granted.

resurrection. A return to life after one has died.

righteous. That which is right in accordance with the Law. The term is particularly used to describe people who are in a right relationship with God through faith.

sacrament. A sacred act instituted by God where there are visible means connected to His Word. In a sacrament God offers, gives, and seals to the individual the forgiveness of sins earned by Christ.

sacrifice. An act of worship where a person presents an offering to God. Sacrifices were practiced from ancient times to atone for sins and to express thankfulness to God. Sacrifices were offered for various purposes. Among the main ones mentioned in the Old Testament are the sin offering, the trespass offering, the burnt offering, the peace offering, the meal and drink offerings, and the heifer offering. Offerings were sacrificed on the altar morning and evening, at each Sabbath and new moon, and at the three leading festivals. All sacrifices point to and are fulfilled in Christ, the Lamb of God, who was sacrificed for the sins of the world.

salvation. Deliverance from any type of evil, both physical and spiritual. Spiritual salvation includes rescue from sin. It is a gift of God's grace through faith in Christ.

Satan. The chief fallen angel and enemy of God, humanity, and all that is good. Sometimes called Abaddon, Apollyon, or Beelzebub.

sin. Sin is both doing what God forbids and failing to do what He commands. Because of sin everyone deserves temporal and eternal death. Only by grace through faith in Christ, who kept God's Law perfectly and suffered the punishment for the sins of the world, does one escape the results of sin.

Son of God. The title is applied to Jesus in a unique sense. It says that Jesus as the Son is equal to God the Father.

Son of Man. Jesus used this title to emphasize the power and dominion He receives from the Ancient of Days. (See Daniel 7 and Matthew 16:27.)

soul, spirit. The soul is not separate from the body; rather, it is that which gives life: it animates the flesh. It is the inner person as distinguished from the flesh. The soul departs at death. It is the seat of the appetites, emotions, and passions. It can be lost and saved.

suffering servant. Jesus is the fulfillment of the suffering servant spoken about in the Old Testament (Isaiah 42:1–4; 52:13–53:12).

tabernacle. The movable sanctuary in the form of a tent.

temple. The fixed sanctuary of the Lord.

testament. *See* covenant.

tithe. A tenth part of one's income. According to the Law, a tenth of all produce of land and herds was sacred to the Lord.

transfiguration. The name given to the time when Jesus was visibly glorified in the presence of His three disciples.

Trinity. The church's term for the coexistence of Father, Son, and Holy Spirit in the unity of the Godhead; three distinct persons in one divine being or essence. The term *Trinity* does not occur in the Bible, but many passages support the doctrine of the Trinity.

unleavened. Bread without yeast. The Israelites ate unleavened bread at Passover as a reminder of the exodus.

will. Inclination or choice. God's will is that which He determines. It is revealed in His acts, His Law, and especially in Christ. Humanity's fallen or natural will cannot will good. God's grace alone is able to incline a person's will to good.

Word. God's Word comes to people in various forms, for example, through speaking, writing, visions, and symbols. Scripture is the Word of God. Jesus Christ is the supreme revelation of God. He is the living Word.

works. Whether a person's works are good or bad depends on that person's relationship to God. Only a person who believes in Jesus Christ as Savior can do good works in God's eyes, since good works are a fruit of faith.

world. Used not only to describe the universe or the human race, but often to denote the wicked and unregenerate—those who are opposed to God.

worship. To bow down, to kiss the hand, to revere, to work for, or to serve. The respect and reverence given to God. New Testament worship is centered on the Word of God. It involves reading Scripture and psalms, singing hymns and spiritual songs, teaching, praying, and celebrating the Lord's Supper.